# 110 Nature Hot Spots in MANITOBA and SASKATCHEWAN

# 110 Nature Hot Spots in

# MANITOBA and SASKATCHEWAN

## The Best Parks, Conservation Areas and Wild Places

Jenn Smith Nelson and Doug O'Neill

FIREFLY BOOKS

## A FIREFLY BOOK

Published by Firefly Books Ltd. 2019

First printing

Library of Congress Control Number: 2018961514

Library and Archives Canada Cataloguing in Publication
Smith Nelson, Jenn, 1976-, author
    110 nature hot spots in Manitoba and Saskatchewan : the best parks,
conservation areas and wild places / Jenn Smith Nelson, Doug O'Neill.

Includes index.
ISBN 978-0-228-10169-7 (softcover)

    1. Natural areas--Manitoba--Guidebooks. 2. Natural areas--Saskatchewan-
-Guidebooks. 3. Parks--Manitoba--Guidebooks. 4. Parks--Saskatchewan-
-Guidebooks. 5. Protected areas--Manitoba--Guidebooks. 6. Protected
areas--Saskatchewan--Guidebooks. 7. Manitoba--Description and travel.
8. Saskatchewan  Description and travel. 9. Manitoba--Guidebooks. 10.
Saskatchewan--Guidebooks. 11. Guidebooks. I. O'Neill, Doug, 1959-, author
II. Title. III. Title: One hundred ten nature hot spots in Manitoba and
Saskatchewan.

FC3233.S65 2019          917.1204          C2018-905976-1

Published in the United States by
Firefly Books (U.S.) Inc.
P.O. Box 1338, Ellicott Station
Buffalo, New York  14205

Published in Canada by
Firefly Books Ltd.
50 Staples Avenue, Unit 1
Richmond Hill, Ontario  L4B 0A7

Cover and interior design: Noor Majeed
Maps: George Walker

Printed in China

Canada ▮ We acknowledge the financial support
of the Government of Canada.

Disclaimer: This book is for
information purposes only.
The authors and publisher have
tried their best to ensure the accu-
racy of the information in this
book. Trail conditions and habitats
may change over time. Seasonal
and natural influences as well as
human-made and animal-made
obstructions or alterations to
the trails may change or affect
the conditions described in this
book. The authors and publisher
are not responsible for any thefts,
problems, injuries or accidental
misfortunes from use of the
information contained in this
book. Please remember that safety
is a personal responsibility.

# Dedication

To my mom, Eva, my sons, Finn and Zevin,
and Jamie — who all provided me the time,
support, love and patience to write this book.
— J.S.N.

I'd like to dedicate my contribution to my
late father, Leo O'Neill, whose sole release
while singlehandedly raising eight kids
was a ramble through a snow-filled forest
or an afternoon escape along a tree-lined
country lane. Intentionally or otherwise, he
instilled in me a profound love of nature.
— D.O.

The Great Sand Hills, Saskatchewan

Previous pages: Caribou River
Provincial Wilderness Park, Manitoba

Clearwater Lake Provincial
Park, Manitoba

# Contents

# Introduction

Never has there been a more crucial time to connect with nature. Newscasts and social media feeds are filled with video clips of disappearing ice floes, reports on the ever-mounting ill effects of global warming and heart-rending stories detailing yet one more species at risk. Of course, there are good news stories: conservationists who've poured their efforts into protecting endangered species, the return of wildlife to abandoned habitats, the revitalization of once-polluted waterways and the restoration of wetlands. The recent reintroduction of plains bison to parts of Western Canada is just one shining example of nature conservation at its best. Dovetailing these stories is an increasing amount of airtime and digital space chronicling the healing power of nature and how vital it is to get outdoors and connect with nature's life cycles, to immerse ourselves in the wild amid flora and fauna.

This call to nature is by no means reserved for botanists, biologists and environmentalists. Nature's wonders — or nature hot spots, as we call them — are there for all of us. In connecting with nature we heal, learn and thrive.

It was this call to nature that initially drew us to explore and, later, write about the incredible nature hot spots of Saskatchewan and Manitoba.

Saskatchewan's natural attributes and diversity consistently surprise visitors and residents alike. The province is often associated with flat agricultural land, but in reality it's bursting with natural gems: diverse wildlife (especially birds), craggy badlands, rolling hills, sand dunes, lush boreal forests, endless northern waterways and, of course, that iconic sky.

Manitoba, like Saskatchewan, is full of its share of rewarding recreational experiences — from canoeing through labyrinths of exposed Canadian Shield to hiking to the highest peak in the Manitoba Escarpment. The province also hosts some of the world's most spectacular nature-viewing opportunities. Polar bear watching, kayaking with beluga whales and witnessing the fall migration of hundreds of Canada geese are all activities that await nature enthusiasts in Manitoba.

We've tried our best to compile in one volume the very best nature hot spots and experiences these two amazing provinces offer (as well as a handful of highlights from Northwestern Ontario, close to the Manitoba border), and we hope our efforts inspire many healing journeys into the great outdoors.

Of course, a successful trip into nature requires a degree of practical planning as well as an understanding of the risks. Like in all natural spaces, some of which may be very remote or ecologically fragile, you should exercise caution and care — both to protect yourself and the flora and fauna you're admiring.

In this book we've given you a fairly broad outline of what to expect at each location, but if you have specific needs or questions, you should call the site or managing office ahead of time. We urge hikers to follow common rules for hiker safety: always carry 2 litres of water, dress in layers, pack enough food in case of unexpected delays and let someone know your hiking route — especially if you hike alone. Map-reading and compass skills can also get you and your fellow hikers out of challenging situations. When hiking near waterfalls, water bodies or ice-covered rocks and trails, be mindful of slippery surfaces. If you're backcountry camping, rely on previously used campsites to minimize your disturbance of the terrain. Paddlers should do a thorough assessment of rapids, water depths and lengths of portages before embarking. As well, novice kayakers and canoeists should never attempt routes better suited for more experienced paddlers. Wherever possible stick to established routes and trails and respect wildlife habitats. As the saying goes, "Take only memories and leave only footprints."

Always give wild animals their space, especially during birthing and mating seasons. Stay at least 30 metres away from species such as deer, elk and moose and 100 metres away from species such as bears, wolves and bison. (Bears are common throughout both Manitoba and Saskatchewan. Information on Bear SMART guidelines is available through most park and natural resources offices.) Getting too close to animals, large or small, can have dire consequences. Though some animals may seem docile, remember they are still wild and their behaviour cannot be predicted. Quick movements and loud noises can also be frightening and stressful to wildlife, so tread quietly. Lastly, never pick up or feed wild animals.

Following these practices will ensure you enjoy your time exploring these nature hot spots and that there will still be nature hot spots to explore tomorrow.

## Nature Hot Spots and Dogs

Given the delicate nature of many of these destinations, we strongly recommend that you leave your pets at home. Even the most well-behaved dogs are capable of disrupting a sensitive ecosystem, and their presence and excrement may attract dangerous wildlife or scare animals away, which could affect your wildlife-watching experience. If you wish to bring your dog, please contact the destination in advance to learn about limitations and any precautions you must take. Please obey all signs, dispose of your pet's excrement appropriately and take additional care when meeting other people and pets.

## Icon Legend

These icons appear throughout to give you an idea of the available activities and features at each hot spot.

🚶 **Hiking**

🔭 **Wildlife viewing**

🚴 **Cycling**

🎣 **Fishing**

🏇 **Horseback riding**

🚣 **Paddling**

🛥 **Power boating**

⛵ **Sailing**

🏊 **Swimming**

🤿 **Scuba diving or snorkelling**

⛷ **Cross-country skiing**

🏂 **Snowshoeing**

🛷 **Snowmobiling**

⛺ **Camping**

🔭 **Stargazing**

🦕 **Fossil hunting**

♿ **Accessible**

Information regarding universal access has been taken from available data provided by each location. Please note that this data may refer to specific trails, parking or toilets at the hot spot, and visitors with accessibility needs may be unable to experience fully the highlights we profile. Please confirm the availability of accessible facilities and trails prior to departure.

# Welcome to Manitoba

"Keep close to Nature's heart," wrote early environmentalist John Muir, who spent his formative years exploring nature spots in Canada, "and break clear away once in a while, and climb a mountain or spend a week in the woods. Wash your spirit clean."

Keeping close to Nature's heart is relatively easy in Manitoba. I discovered that on my first visit to the Prairie province in my second year of university. I was westward-bound from Ontario to spend the summer in Western Canada and an unexpected train delay gave me the option of spending a few days in Manitoba. I joined a band of like-minded backpackers (with limited cash) and together we cobbled together enough money to rent a car and head to Whiteshell Provincial Park.

It was the pink granite cliffs that grabbed my attention. I was expecting prairie — flat fields of golden wheat that extended as far as the eye could see. The sandy beaches and waterfalls were equally surprising. But that's what nature travel is all about, isn't it? To explore unknown terrain, to quash preconceived notions, to stare at unfamiliar landforms, to gaze dumbfounded at rare animal species and other curios of nature.

During my countless travels through the province, I've become enamored with the natural wonders of Manitoba, which in Cree means "the narrows of the Great Spirit" or "where the spirit lives." Selecting which natural wonders to highlight in this book was challenging. Readers will notice that quite a few — but not all — of Manitoba's 92 provincial parks are included. And its 100,000 lakes? Some get special treatment, others merit a passing reference, but clearly not all of them could fit into these pages. Overall, my guiding principle for this project was to focus on nature hot spots that offer a unique point of interest, such as special flora and fauna or curious landforms, or were the result of some natural phenomenon. I also included a handful of nature hot spots in northwestern Ontario that are ecologically interesting places already frequented by Manitobans. (Who knew there were so many American white pelicans in Lake of the Woods?)

Some places were never up for debate. For instance, Riding Mountain National Park was included because not only is it one of the crown jewels of our national parks system, but also it contains not one but three distinct ecosystems — a rarity in the natural world. Churchill, renowned for its polar bears, beluga whales and the northern lights, was also a shoo-in. I flagged the 4,000-hectare Little Limestone Lake, one of the most colourful lakes in Manitoba, because of its status as the largest marl lake in the world. Visitors with some time on their hands can watch the calcite-rich water change from brilliant turquoise in the morning to a robin's egg blue by the afternoon. Manitoba's 500-kilometre Pine to Prairie International Birding Trail warranted an entry of its own because it's an easy-to-follow route for birders that offers a chance to observe endangered species, such as the piping plover. Outdoor enthusiasts can expect scores of other surprises in the following pages.

I hope this book inspires you to break away and explore the nature hot spots of Manitoba and, in doing so, get closer to Nature's heart.

– Doug O'Neill

→ **An expedition to view polar bears in Churchill is one of the area's biggest draws.**

**2**

366 10

**5**

366

**10**

• Dauphin

5

Wasagaming •

16   **10**   5   Sandy Bay •   *Lake Manitoba*

Minnedosa •

Neepawa •   50

Virden •   Portage la Prairie   6   Stonewall

1   Brandon •   34   1   **7**   Winnipeg

83   **12**   *Assiniboine R.*   3   Lorette •

*Souris R.*   Carman •   • Ste. Anne

10   5   59   • Niverville

elita •   75   • Steinbach

**13**   3   • Killarney   3   Winkler   *Red R.*

Morden  Altona

• Peguis   *Bloodvein R.*

6   304

**3**

7   *Lake Winnipeg*

**5**   Narcisse •   Gimli •

17   11

9   59   12

8   317   315   *Winnipeg*

Selkirk •   Lac du Bonnet •

• Beausejour   44

1   **14**

302   15   1

12

**9**

USA

# Southern Manitoba and Kenora District

# Birds Hill Provincial Park

**Just a 25-minute drive from downtown Winnipeg, this park is home to one of the largest populations of white-tailed deer in North America**

## What Makes This Hot Spot Hot?

- A rarity (perhaps even oddity) in Manitoba exists here: a cedar bog.
- Hiking trails cater to specific natural elements found in the park, such as the cedar bog, white-tailed deer, chickadees and burr oak trees.
- The park is home to 450 white-tailed deer.

**Address:** Provincial Trunk Hwy 59, 24 km northeast of Winnipeg, MB
**GPS:** 50.02757; −96.88704
**Tel:** (1-800) 214-6497
**Website:** gov.mb.ca/sd/parks

**Open year-round**

♿ (Check ahead)

↗ **The white-tailed deer is known for flipping its tail as it dashes away, revealing a stark white underside, hence the name.**

Hike. Trek. Ramble. Then stop and listen. That's the best way to experience the hidden (and not-so-hidden) wonders of Birds Hill Provincial Park — with feet planted firmly on the ground, eyes and ears attuned to the surrounding landscape.

Lest the name suggests this is a go-to destination exclusively for birders, Birds Hill Provincial Park was named after Dr. Curtis Bird, the first speaker of the Manitoba provincial legislature. There are, of course, plenty of songbirds, waterfowl and other species should you be looking for birding opportunities.

The 35-square-kilometre park encompasses glacier-formed hills and ridges where visitors can explore aspen and oak forests, open prairie, savannah, spruce groves, mixed boreal forests and, surprisingly, a cedar bog, which is rare in Manitoba. Dense stands of eastern white cedar provide a thick canopy that blocks the sunlight from reaching the sponge-like peat on the floor of the bog, which is typically wet and muddy. These protected, somewhat hidden, nature spots are favoured by white-tailed deer.

Themed hiking trails include the 3.5-kilometre Cedar Bog Self-Guiding Trail, which crosses through grasslands, stands of aspen and oak trees and, of course, eastern white

cedar. Along this route you'll see Canada's largest population of western silvery aster, a perennial wildflower and now a protected species. It's found in only three places in Manitoba — Birds Hill Provincial Park being one of them. In winter, on this same trail, you'll encounter blue jays, pine grosbeaks, hairy woodpeckers and black-capped chickadees. With snow on the ground, it's easier to spot signs of white-tailed deer, snowshoe hares, squirrels, mice and voles.

The 1.5-kilometre White-Tailed Deer Trail (sometimes called Pine Ridge Trail) is an ideal way to learn about the behaviour, habitat and biology of the white-tailed deer living in the park. White-tailed deer can leap 9 metres horizontally and 2.5 metres vertically and reach speeds of up to 58 kilometres an hour. Dawn and dusk are the best times to see the deer. Other favourite themed trails include the Chickadee Trail and Bur Oak Self-Guiding Trail.

The most popular human-made attraction is Kingfisher Lake, which is ideal for swimming and other watersports. There are also picnic sites, a campground, a riding stable, a restaurant and a store.

If the music of songbirds doesn't appeal, in July there's the annual Winnipeg Folk Festival, which the park has hosted since 1974.

↑ Glacier-formed hills, ridges and open prairie make up much of the terrain of this 35-square-kilometre park.

↓ The western silvery aster is a threatened flower and considered rare in Canada.

# Duck Mountain Provincial Park

*One of the biggest draws to Duck Mountain Provincial Park is Baldy Mountain, the highest point in Manitoba*

## What Makes This Hot Spot Hot?

- An observation tower atop Baldy Mountain — the highest elevation point in the province — offers spectacular views of the surrounding landscape.
- The waters of the spring-fed East Blue Lake are so clear that you can see 12 to 18 metres to the bottom.
- The 1,400-square-kilometre park is home to a diversity of fish and other wildlife.

**Address:** Provincial Rd 366, 35 km north of Provincial Trunk Hwy 5
**GPS:** 51.59572; –100.91052
**Tel:** (204) 945-6784
**Website:** gov.mb.ca/sd/parks

**Open year-round**

 

&#9855; (Check ahead)

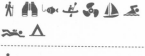
↗ **Dragonflies, like the belted whiteface, benefit from Duck Mountain's wetlands and rolling woodlands.**

While there are plenty of waterfowl, don't come expecting to see an overabundance of ducks. Duck Mountain Provincial Park boasts a diversity of flora and fauna that are attracted to the wetlands, rolling woodlands, valley meadows and many spring-fed lakes. The Duck Mountains appeared about 10,000 to 12,000 years ago, unearthed by retreating glaciers, and now constitute one segment of the Manitoba Escarpment, which incorporates numerous ecosystems and landscapes.

The Duck Mountains — or "the Ducks" as they're affectionately known by Manitobans — stand in contrast to the fairly flat Manitoba prairie. Consequently, many visitors (and lots of residents) make a point of heading up Baldy Mountain, which, at 831 metres above sea level, is the highest point in the entire province. Atop the mountain is a 12-metre observation tower that is accessible by car or by following the Baldy Mountain Viewing Tower Trail. Hikers should be cautious, as the trail is steep in a few spots, but the views up top are worth the effort.

The park's spring-fed lakes,

of which East Blue Lake is the clearest and most well known, include Blue Lake, Wellman Lake, Singush Lake and Childs Lake. They're popular with campers and nature lovers looking for birds, like the common loon, as well as anglers who come for the walleye, yellow perch, lake whitefish, northern pike, muskellunge and trout (including rainbow, brook, speckled, brown and lake varieties).

There are plenty of canoe routes to paddle. The 6.4-kilometre Beaver Lake Canoe Route is accessible south of Glad Lake or from Beaver Lake, off Pine River Road in the northern section of the park.

Scuba divers are especially drawn to East and West Blue lakes and Childs Lake because of the clarity of the water.

With a set of binoculars — and lots of patience — you can get decent views of the elk in the park, especially by following the Wapiti Self-Guiding Trail, which begins at the parking lot at the Duck Mountain Forest Centre off Provincial Road 366. The optional loop trail off the main trail passes near the elks' feeding ground.

**Note:** Don't confuse this park with the identically named Duck Mountain Provincial Park across the border in Saskatchewan.

↑ Birdwatching, canoeing and fishing are popular pastimes on the numerous spring-fed lakes within Duck Mountain Provincial Park.

↓ A common loon displays on Childs Lake. Environmentalists have undertaken steps to protect the loon at Duck Mountain.

HECLA/GRINDSTONE PROVINCIAL PARK

# Grassy Narrows Marsh

*Embrace the wonders of marsh life: boreal chorus frogs, bald eagles, moose, Canada geese and plenty of waterfowl*

## What Makes This Hot Spot Hot?

- Visitors can learn about the vital role of marshes along 25 kilometres of hiking trails.
- Evening concerts in the marsh feature boreal chorus frogs.
- Birders can witness the fall migrations of Canada geese, bald eagles and other waterfowl.

**Address:** Hecla/Grindstone Provincial Park, 165 km north of Winnipeg on Provincial Trunk Hwy 8
**GPS:** 51.04528; −96.83521
**Tel:** (1-800) 214-6497
**Website:** gov.mb.ca/sd/parks

**Open year-round**

♿ (Limited, check ahead)

↗ The sound of the boreal chorus frog's breeding call fills the evenings in early spring.

Marshes often get a bad rap. They've long been misunderstood habitats, dismissed as nothing but breeding grounds for mosquitoes and pestilence. But marshes play a vital role in the environmental health of a region, filtering the water, providing habitat for specific types of waterfowl and animals and absorbing floodwaters — which means they are crucial for flood management.

Marshes often have a greater variety of flora and fauna than can be found in forests or lakes, and in terms of biological productivity, they are second only to tropical rainforests.

The Grassy Narrows Marsh, a rehabilitated and managed marsh on the channel between Hecla Island and the mainland, has become an important nesting area for Canada geese and other waterfowl. Cross the causeway to access the Grassy Narrows Marsh Trail, which winds for about 25 kilometres through the protected wetland.

The venerable conservancy group Ducks Unlimited Canada gets a lot of the

credit, along with Manitoba Conservation, for establishing a system of dykes to control water levels in this marsh and restore habitat for waterfowl, bald eagles, hawks and moose.

In addition to Canada geese, birders are apt to spot red-necked grebes, American bitterns, great blue herons, yellow warblers and killdeer, among others. Wildlife sightings include beavers, minks, muskrats, shrews, moose, white-tailed deer, red foxes, meadow voles, grey wolves, otters, lynx, snowshoe hares and deer mice.

Keen to listen to nature's music? Early spring is the best time to hear the breeding call of the boreal chorus frog, which has been described as "the sound of drawing your finger down the teeth of a comb." Late day or early evening is optimal.

The best time to see the Canada geese V-formation as they migrate south is between late August and October. Local birders suggest an October visit to observe hundreds of bald eagles during their migration period.

↑ Marshes like Grassy Narrows are second only to tropical rainforests in terms of biological activity.

↓ Grassy Narrows Marsh is an important nesting area for Canada geese.

NORTHWESTERN ONTARIO

# Lake of the Woods Provincial Park

*Prepare to be surprised by a jumble of flora and fauna — including pelicans*

## What Makes This Hot Spot Hot?

- The park sits in a transition zone, where flora that typically grows in the Prairies and southern and northern parts of Ontario converge.
- Colonies of American white pelicans, a surprise species in this area of Canada, occupy the park.
- Lake of the Woods is a popular destination with anglers who fish for walleye, northern pike, perch and many other fish species.

**Address:** Hwy 621, 43 km north of Rainy River, ON
**GPS:** 49.08306; −94.55405
**Tel:** (807) 548-4351, ext. 221
**Website:** ontarioparks.com

**Open year-round; park is non-operational with no facilities**

♿ (Limited, check ahead)

↗ **Stand-up paddleboarding is an increasingly popular way to explore some of the park's 14,522 islands.**

Nature experts sometimes refer to the species that coexist in Lake of the Woods Provincial Park as a "jumble." The explanation is simple. Not only is the remote 20,675-hectare park located near the borders of three divisions (Ontario, Manitoba and Minnesota), it's also situated in an ecological transition zone where plants and trees that typically grow in the Prairies and southern and northern parts of Ontario converge.

That means visitors will see southern hardwoods (like ash, basswood and elm) close to prairie tree species (such as Manitoba maple) and northern trees (including jack pine and northern spruce). The spectacular diversity of animal species reflects the transitioning flora. Birders are apt to see prairie birds (like the yellow-headed blackbird and western meadowlark) and southern winged creatures (such as the Baltimore oriole, scarlet tanager and red-headed woodpecker) all in the same area.

The body of water known as Lake of the Woods is 135 kilometres long and 90 kilometres at its widest point, and it has a shoreline of 40,000 kilometres (100,000 kilometres if you include the area's 14,522 islands).

The extensive shorelines and numerous islands provide a protected habitat for the biggest surprise species in Lake of the Woods Provincial Park: colonies of American white pelicans, one of the largest birds in North America, have taken over several remote islands and waterways as their permanent nesting grounds in the past couple of decades. (Their arrival has meant anglers have more competition for the fish.)

Other bird species include migrating waterfowl, such as American widgeons, pintails and mergansers (who feed in the wild rice bays of the lake) and the piping plover, a species at risk in this part of Ontario. Moose, black bears and deer also inhabit the park, but there's no guarantee you'll spot these creatures due to the vastness of the park and the seemingly infinite number of small islands.

Equally popular in Lake of the Woods is fishing. Anglers are enticed by waters full of walleye, northern pike, perch, sauger, crappie, smallmouth bass, largemouth bass, lake trout, lake sturgeon, whitefish, suckers and muskellunge. The Big Grassy and Onigaming First Nations also fish (and hunt) here, particularly in the southeast corner of the park.

Other ways to explore the water include swimming, canoeing, kayaking, stand-up paddleboarding and powerboating.

Since Lake of the Woods Provincial Park is a non-operational park, there are no facilities or staff. Gear can be acquired from local outfitters, and there are lodges in towns like Rainy River and Nestor Falls for overnight accommodations.

↑ A serene morning scene in the remote 20,675-hectare Lake of the Woods.

↓ Undisturbed shorelines provide protection, and the lakes offer plenty of fish to colonies of American white pelicans.

# Narcisse Snake Dens

*Snakes alive! Four dens are home to over 50,000 red-sided garter snakes that slither about for public viewing each spring and fall*

## What Makes This Hot Spot Hot?

- Visitors can learn about the behavior and life cycles of the red-sided garter snake.
- The dens support the largest gathering of snakes in the world.
- The snakes attract other wildlife to the area, such as bears, hawks and owls.

**Address:** Provincial Trunk Hwy 17, 6 km north of Narcisse, MB
**GPS:** 50.73452; −97.53035
**Tel:** (1-800) 214-6497
**Website:** gov.mb.ca/sd/wildlife

**Open year-round; late April to early May and also early September are the best times for viewing the snakes**

&#9855; **(Check ahead)**

↗ **The red-sided garter snake is harmless but can get agitated if threatened.**

Just as bears awaken and emerge from their winter dens each spring, so too do red-sided garter snakes (*Thamnophis sirtalis infernalis*). In fact, during the spring mating season (which runs from the end of April through the first few weeks of May) and each fall (early September), more than 50,000 snakes occupy the four snake pits at the Narcisse Snake Dens, about a 90-minute drive north of Winnipeg.

These harmless snakes spend the winter in a network of caverns and crevasses in the limestone. Spring — the call to begin mating — prompts

the snakes to leave their dens en masse. It's during this springtime period, especially on sunny days, that visitors can witness the "mating ball," in which one female is surrounded by as many as 100 males.

The four snake dens are connected by an easy-to-follow 3-kilometre interpretive trail through native grassland and aspen forest. The best viewing spots are the observation platforms next to the dens.

If you miss the spring concentration of snakes, or wish to pay another visit, return in early September when the snakes, which can travel anywhere from 12 to 17 kilometres away from the dens, head back to the dens in anticipation of the cold, wet weather.

The naturally formed caverns, which are part of the Narcisse Wildlife Management Area, are appealing to the snakes — as is the local food supply: frogs, leeches, tadpoles, earthworms and rodents. The garter snakes, in turn, become food for black bears, raccoons, skunks and especially birds. In fact, most are picked off by hawks, magpies, crows and owls.

Please note that you are not allowed to enter the dens, which is for the protection of the snakes. They are harmless but can get agitated. Always respect the animals and their habitat, and as with any wildlife viewing experience, do not feed the snakes.

↑ **More than 50,000 snakes leave their limestone caverns in the spring to reproduce and then return en masse each fall.**

# Nopiming Provincial Park

*Nopiming Provincial Park, known for its herd of woodland caribou and rare flowers, presents an opportunity to learn about the rejuvenating effects of forest fires*

## What Makes This Hot Spot Hot?

- In late June, the blue flag iris appears among shoreline grasses while rare orchids flower briefly on the forest floor.
- Hiking trails offer visitors the opportunity to see first-hand the variety of flora and fauna that flourishes decades after a devastating forest fire.
- Roaming the park is a herd of woodland caribou, a rarity in southern Manitoba.

**Address:** Provincial Rd 315, 53 km northeast of Lac du Bonnet, MB
**GPS:** 50.67778; −95.32424
**Tel:** (1-800) 214-6497
**Website:** gov.mb.ca/sd/parks

**Open year-round**

↗ **Blue flag irises are known for growing along the shorelines of lakes, rivers and ponds.**

Earth. Wind. Water. Fire. While all of the parks across Canada, provincial and national, seek to educate visitors about the four elements of nature, Nopiming Provincial Park is unique in that it's a living testament to the role of fire in a natural setting.

On Labour Day weekend 1983, flames from what became known as the Long Lake Fire swept through Nopiming Provincial Park and the surrounding area and decimated 29,138 hectares. Devastating, most certainly, but fire, being a natural part of a forest's life cycle, also played a role in the rejuvenation of this 1,429-square-kilometre section of wilderness. Pick up brochures at the trailhead of the 2-kilometre Fire of 'Eighty-Three Self-Guiding Trail and learn, for instance, about the positive effects of extreme heat on jack pine reproduction and how trembling aspen, considered post-burn pioneers, thrive after a fire.

Another instructional hike worth exploring is the Ancient Mountains Self-Guiding Trail,

which is an ideal way to learn about the ancient mountains that dominated the landscape millions of years ago and were revealed by a study of the rocks left exposed after the 1983 fire.

The wildlife found in Nopiming Provincial Park also bears witness to the impact of fire. For instance, taller trees downed by fire means that shrubs and young aspen are allowed to thrive, which in turn attracts snowshoe hares, white-tailed deer and moose, along with their predators — lynx, coyotes and wolves. Another reason to visit Nopiming Provincial Park is

for a chance to spot a roaming herd of woodland caribou, a species that seldom ventures this far south in Manitoba.

Flora fans often stroll the shoreline grasses in late June to see the blue flag, also called the blue wild iris. Rare orchids have been known to flower briefly on the forest floor in shaded areas.

To visit the remote areas of Nopiming, consider one of the numerous options for overnight canoe trips. Two popular routes are Rabbit River to Cole Lake and Bird River to Elbow Lake. Always check campfire status with park staff before embarking.

↑ Much of the verdant landscape visitors see today in Nopiming Provincial Park is — perhaps surprisingly — the result of a horrendous forest fire in 1983.

→ Coyotes are typically seen in farming areas but also venture into the boreal forest as far north as Thompson.

# Oak Hammock Marsh

*Visitors will learn the true value of underappreciated marshlands*

## What Makes This Hot Spot Hot?

- Oak Hammock Marsh is one of the most productive ecosystems in Canada, unrivalled in its species diversity.
- There are over 300 species of birds found here.
- The well-equipped interpretive centre offers a wide range of hands-on nature workshops and educational programming.

**Address:** 1 Snow Goose Bay (off Provincial Rd 220), Stonewall, MB
**GPS:** 50.17382; −97.13295
**Tel:** (1-888) 506-2774
**Website:** oakhammockmarsh.ca

**Open year-round; extended hours from Wednesdays to Sundays between mid-September and mid-October for fall migration**

&#9855; (Check ahead)

⤢ **The yellow warbler is just one of the 300 species of birds that inhabit this 20-square-kilometre stretch of open wetland.**

In the 1890s, the 470-square-kilometre area of marsh and fen near the southwestern corner of Lake Winnipeg was known as St. Andrew's Bog. Not a very romantic name, but back then marshlands weren't appreciated as the gems of nature that they are. Marshlands were to be drained for agricultural purposes. And so they were.

Luckily, thanks to the preservation efforts of Ducks Unlimited Canada and the Manitoba government, 20 square kilometres of open wetland thrive today at what's now called Oak Hammock Marsh. Forward-thinking conservationists constructed 22 kilometres of earth dykes to restore part of the original marsh.

Wetlands, like Oak Hammock Marsh, are among the most productive ecosystems on earth, second only to rainforests. Such wetlands play an important role in maintaining water quality by filtering sediment and pollutants. They also function as fish and wildlife habitats, store floodwaters and maintain surface water flow during dry spells. What looks like a swampy marsh is often the equivalent of a "biological supermarket," acting as a rich food source.

Oak Hammock Marsh is home to an incredible diversity of species: 300 species of birds; 25 species of mammals; numerous amphibians, reptiles and fish; and countless invertebrates. An excess of 100,000 waterfowl stop at the marsh during their annual migrations, among them snow geese, Canada geese and blue-winged teals. Other birds in transit (some stay for a while) include the yellow rail, Nelson's sparrow and LeConte's sparrow.

Mammals you might spot include squirrels, beavers, rabbits, hares, shrews, deer mice, foxes, wolves, white-tailed deer, badgers, otters and black

bears. Plant life here runs the gamut — from cattails, duckweed, lilies and irises to orchids, willows, dogwood and a wide variety of roses. Fish species include northern pike, white sucker, spottail shiner, common carp, ninespine stickleback, fathead minnow and emerald shiner, to name a few. Fishing is allowed in Oak Hammock Marsh if you have a provincial fishing licence.

There are 30 kilometres of marked trails (gravel paths, wooden boardwalks and earth and grass footpaths), many of which have been constructed on the dykes. The Oak Hammock Interpretive Centre's maps indicate specific areas such as the squirrel colony, duck pond and dragonfly area, all of

which can be reached on foot.

The interpretive centre offers all manner of educational programs, hands-on workshops and interactive exhibits that emphasize the vital role of marshlands and reveal how they are indeed natural treasures.

↑ Staff at the interpretive centre facilitate educational programs and hands-on workshops to teach visitors about the vital role of marshlands.

↖ The skies over Oak Hammock Marsh are filled with over 100,000 winged creatures during annual migrations.

# Pimachiowin Aki UNESCO World Heritage Site

## The first mixed cultural and natural World Heritage Site in Canada

### What Makes This Hot Spot Hot?

- This wilderness area is home to one of the largest herds of woodland caribou south of the Hudson Bay.
- The parks and conservation reserves protect hundreds of animal species, including black bears, beavers, wolves and birds of prey.
- Visitors will find thousands of kilometres of waterways to explore, in addition to world-class fishing and remote wilderness camping.

**Address:** There is no direct road access into the wilderness areas encompassing Pimachiowin Aki. The areas can be accessed by float plane or boat.
**GPS:** n/a
**Tel:** (1-888) 949-1041
**Website:** pimachiowinaki.org

**Open year-round**

Pimachiowin Aki, which is Ojibwe for "the land that gives life," covers 29,040 square kilometres (almost the size of Vancouver Island) of mostly untouched wilderness and is home to one of the largest herds of caribou south of the Hudson Bay. Four First Nations — Bloodvein River, Little Grand Rapids, Pauingassi and Poplar River — led the campaign to have the area designated a World Heritage Site by the United Nations Educational, Scientific and Cultural Organization's (UNESCO) World Heritage Committee. These First Nations communities are integral in the management and care of this unrivalled natural space, which encompasses Atikaki and South Atikaki Provincial Parks in Manitoba and Eagle-Snowshoe Conservation Reserve and Woodland Caribou Provincial Park in Ontario.

### Atikaki Provincial Wilderness Park

Getting into Atikaki Provincial Wilderness Park, which is east of Lake Winnipeg on the Ontario-Manitoba border, takes some planning — such is the case for many remote nature hot spots in Manitoba and northwestern Ontario. There is no direct road access, and the closest community is the Bloodvein First Nation. Charter flights from Winnipeg can be arranged through various outfitters, lodges and air charter companies. One of the more popular water routes starts south of the park at Wallace Lake (which is 250 kilometres from Winnipeg, off Provincial Road 304).

Much of Atikaki remains untouched, and there's a lot of wilderness to explore in this nearly 4,000-square-kilometre park: cliffs, rocky outcrops, rugged forests, countless lakes, waterfalls, cascading rapids and wild rivers.

A herd of caribou (numbering between 300 and 500) inhabits the park. *Atikaki*, the name given to the area by the Ojibwe, means "country of the caribou." Caribou nourish themselves on two types of lichens that are prevalent in the boreal forests in this region: reindeer lichen, which grows all year, and old man's beard, which hangs from mature jack pine trees and is an important food source in the winter. Other wildlife includes elk, moose, loons, bald eagles and black bears.

Atikaki contains some of the warmest and driest environments within Manitoba's boreal forest. This accounts for the appearance of Prairie plants, such as prairie spikemoss and prairie rush, which aren't often found in this region.

The area is known for its

fabulous paddling opportunities, including whitewater rafting. Popular canoe routes follow the Bloodvein Canadian Heritage, Pigeon, Gammon and Leyond rivers. Fishing is also a common pastime on the water, luring in anglers looking to catch walleye, northern pike and lake trout.

For more information, visit gov.mb.ca/sd/parks.

↑ Atikaki lures anglers with the promise of catching fish, like northern pike and lake trout.

↖ Moose are one of the most frequent wildlife sightings in Atikaki Provincial Wilderness Park.

↑ The sun sets on Eagle Lake in Eagle-Snowshoe Conservation Reserve.

↗ Woodland Caribou Provincial Park has 1,500 fairly primitive canoe-in campsites for paddlers going the distance.

→ South Atikaki is one of the few places in Manitoba where the American wintergreen grows.

↘ Swamp pink, which blooms in early spring, is rarely — if ever — spotted elsewhere in Manitoba other than South Atikaki.

## Eagle-Snowshoe Conservation Reserve

The Eagle-Snowshoe Conservation Reserve is a protected domain about 95 kilometres northwest of Kenora, Ontario, and includes the area along the Ontario-Manitoba border from Snowshoe Lake to Eagle Lake.

This conservation reserve plays a vital role in the protection of woodland caribou. Not only does the reserve provide a safe habitat for this species, but also there are several important calving and nursery areas along the corridor from Eagle Lake to Chase Lake. The reserve is also committed to protecting its beavers, otters, martens, moose, black bears and white-tailed deer.

The terrain is typical Canadian Shield — a glaciated landscape marked by elongated lake systems, bedrock, sudden drops in elevation and thin soil, in which birch, poplar, spruce, balsam fir and jack pine grow. Other plant life includes mosses, shrubs, ferns and fungi.

Fishing for walleye, northern pike and lake trout is one of the primary activities in this conservation reserve. Fishing expeditions can be arranged through outfitters in Kenora. The area is also popular for those who like to canoe, hunt, wilderness camp and, in the winter, snowmobile. Most visitors rely on fly-in transportation. Backcountry canoeists keen on long-distance routes should consult local outfitters before departing.

## South Atikaki Provincial Park

South Atikaki Provincial Park was originally part of Atikaki

Provincial Park before becoming its own separate entity in 1997 and then a designated provincial park in 2003. The park fulfills an important role in eastern Manitoba — the protection of woodland caribou. According to wildlife experts, there are two caribou herds in the vicinity of the park: the Atikaki-Berens herd and the Owl-Flinstone herd. Other wildlife includes moose, wolves, lynx, beavers, black bears, loons, bald eagles and other birds. Walleye, northern pike and lake trout are the main fish species found in the rivers.

While the plants and trees are typical of the boreal forest (black spruce, jack pine, trembling aspen, balsam poplar, white birch, white spruce and balsam fir), there are a number of uncommon plants in the park, such as rattlesnake manna grass, running pine, sensitive fern, fowl manna grass, American wintergreen, dwarf huckleberry, swamp pink, Hooker's orchid, long-spurred violet and round-leaved bog orchid.

Primary activities during the summer season are canoeing, powerboating, camping, fishing and hunting. Wallace and Siderock lakes attract snowmobilers in the winter months.

South Atikaki Provincial Park is about 25 kilometres from the town of Bissett and 175 kilometres northeast of Winnipeg, sandwiched between Wallace Lake and Atikaki provincial parks. South Atikaki is not accessible by road, but you can reach the park by boat from Wallace Lake or by float plane.

For more information, visit gov.mb.ca/sd/parks.

## Woodland Caribou Provincial Park

During the summer, canoeists seem as plentiful as caribou in Woodland Caribou Provincial Park, but luckily there's plenty of room for both groups in this 450,000-hectare wilderness in northwestern Ontario, close to the Manitoba border. The park's remote, largely untouched boreal forest is an ideal home for what is believed to be one of the largest groups of woodland caribou south of the Hudson Bay. Numbers sometimes reach 200 in a single group.

If you're a paddler, you can choose from approximately 2,000 kilometres of canoe routes on the numerous rivers and lakes within the park. The two major river systems popular with canoeists are the Gammon River and the Bloodvein Heritage River. Paddlers should be experienced in long-distance canoe trips and be prepared to portage. There are about 1,500 fairly primitive canoe-in campsites, which require permits. Canoeists must follow proper backcountry etiquette. If a campsite is full, move on, and minimize human impact on the environment by packing out all that you pack in.

Visiting anglers fish for walleye, northern pike and lake trout, as do the Indigenous Peoples who've long inhabited this region, which is part of their ancestral home. There are ancient Ojibwe pictographs, or rock paintings, throughout the park that must be treated with dignity and respect. Some pictographs depict humans (possibly shamans), while others appear to be variations of caribou and even mystical serpent-like creatures.

If you bring along binoculars, you stand a good chance of spotting great grey owls as well as bald eagles, hawks, waterfowl and nesting songbirds.

Most visitors arrive by boat or float plane directly from Red Lake, Ontario, where the park office and various outfitters are located. For more information, visit ontarioparks.com.

↑ Ancient pictographs are highly valued elements of Indigenous culture and should be treated with respect.

← From a float plane, you can begin to appreciate the vastness of the 450,000-hectare Woodland Caribou Provincial Park.

# Pine to Prairie International Birding Trail

*A lengthy yet rewarding road trip designed for birders*

## What Makes This Hot Spot Hot?

- There are 23 designated birding stops along this nearly 500-kilometre route.
- The International Birding Trail passes through several major nature and wildlife areas, including Oak Hammock Marsh, Whiteshell Provincial Park and Hecla/Grindstone Provincial Park.
- Manitoba sits within three migration corridors where almost 400 species of birds have been recorded.

**Address:** Many start in Buffalo Point, MB, which sits just north of the Canada-U.S. border
**GPS:** n/a
**Tel:** (204) 943-9029
**Website:** gov.mb.ca/watchablewildlife/birding

**Open year-round**

&#9855; **(Varies, check ahead)**

"In order to see birds it is necessary to become a part of the silence," wrote Irish writer Robert Lynd. Birds and prairie silence — both are bountiful in Manitoba.

Manitoba's Pine to Prairie International Birding Trail, which travels almost 500 kilometres across southern Manitoba, is an extension of the International Pine to Prairie Birding Trail south of the border in Minnesota. Starting at Buffalo Point, just north of the Canada-U.S. border, the trail comprises 23 recognized sites frequented or inhabited by specific bird species.

The trail is popular with birders who want to see the great grey owl, the official bird of Manitoba, along with other sought-after species (some of them endangered), such as the Connecticut warbler, spruce grouse, yellow rail, black-backed woodpecker, American three-toed woodpecker and Blackburnian warbler.

It's typical to drive through a range of habitats in a single day, from boreal forest and tall grass to mixed-grass prairies and aspen-oak parkland. The sites along the route include Whiteshell Provincial Park (known for sightings of boreal woodpeckers), Grand Beach Provincial Park (where endangered piping plovers can be seen from mid-May to mid-August) and Tall Grass Prairie Preserve (which is favoured by the western meadowlark and LeConte's sparrow).

The best time to hit the trail? Depends on which birds you want to see. From mid-March to April, significant numbers of waterfowl and raptors migrate through southern Manitoba. April and May are the months to observe breeding waterfowl as well as watch male spruce grouse show off by beating their wings and making deep, drumming sounds. (This is also the season for watching owls at night.) Usually between September and November, raptors migrate along the west shore of Lake Winnipeg. The trail is also popular in winter when woodpeckers, winter finches, owls and other bird species are out and fairly easy to spot.

For more information about the trail and individual stops, download a detailed (and free) pamphlet from the website listed on the opposite page.

↖ The Blackburnian warbler, a fairly common bird on the trail, is one of the easiest warblers to identify because of its orange throat.

↗ The great grey owl is highly sought-after by birders around the world and is one of the reasons many bird enthusiasts follow the Pine to Prairie International Birding Trail.

↪ The male spruce grouse puts on a show during breeding season by beating his wings and making deep, drumming sounds.

# Riding Mountain National Park

*One of Canada's most-visited national parks, with 3,000 square kilometres of protected land where bison roam and 233 kinds of birds and 60 mammal species thrive*

## What Makes This Hot Spot Hot?

- The park, sitting 500 metres above the surrounding prairies, contains three distinct ecosystems: grasslands, upland boreal forest and eastern deciduous forest.
- Abundant birdwatching opportunities can be had at serene Lake Katherine.
- Visitors can get up close to one of Canada's few remaining bison herds, at the Lake Audy Bison Enclosure.

**Address:** 133 Wasagaming Dr, Onanole, MB
**GPS:** 50.65757; −99.97232
**Tel:** (204) 848-7275
**Websites:** pc.gc.ca/en/pn-np, rmbr.ca

**Open year-round; some services and facilities in Wasagaming shut down during the fall and winter**

&#9855; (Check ahead)

When it comes to the curative powers of nature, few places rival Riding Mountain National Park, the 3,000-square-kilometre "island" of wilderness in southwestern Manitoba. It's near impossible to visit the park without experiencing a connectedness with nature — that almost indescribable sense of being at one with the lakes, trees, rolling terrain and wildlife that dwell therein.

Nature has bestowed unique attributes upon Riding Mountain National Park, which sits within the traditional territory of the Anishinaabe Peoples. Chief among them, the park contains three distinct ecosystems within its boundaries: grasslands, upland boreal forest and eastern deciduous forest. That in itself is rare, and it means distinct plant and animal life thrive in each of the park's ecosystems. In 1986 UNESCO designated the wilderness park and the surrounding area a Biosphere Reserve.

Riding Mountain is not a

↑ Riding Mountain contains three distinct ecosystems — grasslands, upland boreal forest and eastern deciduous forest — making for a huge diversity of flora, fauna and serene panoramas.

→ There are over 400 kilometres of trails within the boundaries of Riding Mountain.

↖ Moose, whose numbers in the park total around 3,000, are quite easily spotted during fall and winter, especially in the Moon Lake area.

↑ **In addition to moose, white-tailed deer, elk, bison and other wildlife, there are also black bears in Riding Mountain National Park.**

mountain in the traditional sense, but the park does sit on the Manitoba Escarpment, putting it at 457 metres above the surrounding Manitoban farmland. Within the park is a protected herd of bison, one of the few in Canada. Lending yet another unique dimension to Riding Mountain National Park is that it's one of only five national parks in Canada with a townsite within its borders: Wasagaming, on the shores of Clear Lake, 97 kilometres north of Brandon. That's where the Parks Canada office is located — in a rustic log-constructed building from the 1930s. You might choose to base your exploration of the park from this townsite.

Wildlife is plentiful. There are more than 233 species of birds, at least 60 kinds of mammals, six types of amphibians and 27 fish species, not to mention 69 species of butterflies. Visitors frequently see moose, beavers, porcupines, white-tailed deer, snowshoe hares and elk. Other creatures, such as cougars, are more elusive. Riding Mountain is home to one of the largest populations of black bears in North America. And, of course, there's the Lake Audy Bison Enclosure within the park, which protects a herd of 40 plains bison.

Endangered birds, such as the loggerhead shrike and golden-winged warbler, have surfaced in the park. The trumpeter swan, known for its graceful moves on the water — and rarely seen in Manitoba — nests within the park's boundaries.

A staggering 669 species of plants are found in the park. Among them, the most common trees are poplar, white birch, American elm, Manitoba maple, white spruce, balsam fir, jack pine, black spruce, tamarack and burr oak.

Some of the best ways to observe nature include hiking, horseback riding and biking. Fat biking (sometimes referred to as snow biking) has become a popular year-round trail activity, too. There are more than 400 kilometres of hiking and riding trails. Most are clearly marked and easy to follow, while others are better suited for experienced back-country hikers. Hikers can opt for one of the relatively easy,

↑ Many of the sites within Riding Mountain National Park, such as the Lake Audy Bison Enclosure, are open year-round.

self-guided trails that start on the outskirts of Wasagaming, such as the Clear Lake Trail. For those keen to tackle a more challenging hike, there are backcountry trails, such as the 25-kilometre Birdtail Trail in the northwest corner of the park near Bob Hill Lake.

While many of the services in Wasagaming shut down during winter months, some stay open to cater to winter-time visitors who come to snowshoe, cross-country ski and track animals over the snow.

The large campsite at Clear Lake in Wasagaming makes it relatively easy for nature lovers to spend a few days (or longer) in Riding Mountain National Park. For a fully immersive nature experi-ence, check out the various Parks Canada options, from traditional campsites, yurts and Micro-Cubes (a 10-metre-square cube with a panoramic window) to backcountry sites. Riding Mountain also offers a winter camping program.

Other diversions are plentiful: fishing, boating (check with Parks Canada for any restrictions on motorized

↑ **Birders will likely hear — sooner than they see — the evening grosbeak, which is known to use a variety of sounds.**

boats), kayaking, canoeing, sailing, swimming, scuba diving (especially at Clear Lake) and other activities await at Riding Mountain.

## Lake Katherine

Solitude, peace and silence are ideal conditions to connect with nature. Apart from the wind rippling through the trembling aspen, there's little noise or drama about Lake Katherine, a former Indigenous settlement. Motorized boats are prohibited on the 27-hectare lake, which is located within the traditional territory of the Anishinaabe Peoples. The firepit and a couple of outdoor structures at the lakeside campground are reminders of the First Nations Interpretive Camp that operated at Lake Katherine until 2000.

The relative calm of the lake makes it easier to spot birds, which are attracted to the surrounding boreal forests: yellow-bellied sapsuckers, Philadelphia vireos, myrtle warblers, American redstarts, chestnut-sided warblers and boreal chickadees. The elusive Connecticut warbler has also been sighted, as have the Tennessee, Nashville and Cape May warblers. Your birdwatching retreat won't be completely tranquil, though. The evening grosbeak is known to use a variety of sounds to express anger, surprise, fear, pain,

curiosity and alarm.

There are a handful of fairly easy, level hiking trails, which are also used by horses. The 2.5-kilometre Loon's Island Trail passes through mature aspen and mixed-wood forests along the east side of the lake. Hikers can easily add on the shorter 1.6-kilometre Evergreen Trail, which loops around the north side.

The "no motorboats" rule is a boon to anglers, since there are no revving engines to scare off pike, perch, rainbow and brook trout.

## Lake Audy Bison Enclosure

Within the 3,000-square-kilometre island of wilderness that constitutes Riding Mountain National Park sits another wildlife treasure: a protected herd of 40 or so plains bison in what's known as the Lake Audy Bison Enclosure, a 500-hectare fenced area that can be toured by vehicle only.

Prior to the arrival of Europeans in North America, plains bison numbered 30 million. A combination of factors, primarily the European demand for furs and the advent of the railway, which brought tens of thousands of settlers into the west, led to the rapid decimation of the bison. By the late 1800s, the massive shaggy brown animals had disappeared from Canada.

In 1931, in an attempt to

↑ There are viewing platforms within the Lake Audy Bison Enclosure so that visitors can safely snap a picture of the park's marquis species.

re-establish bison in Manitoba, a herd of 20 were introduced to the Riding Mountain area, which had once been home to the bison. Sadly, bovine tuberculosis, contracted from grazing cows, wiped out the original group. That herd was replaced in 1940 by another 10 bison from Elk Island National Park in Alberta, and the 40 creatures that captivate visitors today are their descendants. Adult males weigh over 730 kilograms, and the females, who give birth between March and May, average 440 kilograms.

The resident bison roam the enclosure, which is divided into winter and summer pastures. Only visitors in vehicles (private cars or compact tour buses and vans) can tour the entire area. You can exit your vehicle and climb a raised viewing deck where the Bison and Grasslands Exhibit details the natural history of bison and the native grasslands.

In the fall, the Lake Audy Bison Enclosure is an excellent place to observe elk in the wild. Experienced guides will sometimes demonstrate elk bugling on homemade bugles. Real elk bugling, when bull elk call out to each other claiming their territory, heats up during mating season, from late August to late September. (Ask for more information at the Parks Canada office in Wasagaming.)

NORTHWESTERN ONTARIO

# Rushing River Provincial Park

*As the name implies, this is your go-to spot to see — and hear — rushing rapids*

## What Makes This Hot Spot Hot?

- The park's rapids cascade over glacier-carved rocks in a dramatic display and provide one of nature's best audio tracks.
- The park is considered the gateway to the popular canoe routes of Eagle-Dogtooth Provincial Park.
- Large groups of loons nest in the park.

**Address:** Hwy 71, 30 km east of Kenora, ON
**GPS:** 49.68158; −94.23582
**Tel:** (807) 548-4351
**Website:** ontarioparks.com

**Open year-round; camping is available mid-May to mid-September**

♿ (Limited, check ahead)

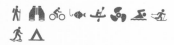

↗ **Dogtooth Lake is popular with birdwatchers, campers, swimmers, anglers and paddlers.**

Lots of Winnipeggers make the 2.5-hour journey to Rushing River Provincial Park in northwestern Ontario. The thunderous rapids, where the waters of Dogtooth Lake spill into Blindfold Lake, are enough to entice nature lovers to visit. This spectacle is thanks to the glacier-carved rocks lining the river, which is easily navigable beyond the rapids.

For those looking for a quieter respite, there are also four sandy beaches in the park, which appeal to vacationing families who want to canoe and swim when they're not hiking or biking.

A variety of marked trails make for excellent nature walks, on which you're likely to see deer, bald eagles and foxes. The 2.7-kilometre Granite Knoll Trail follows the shoreline of Dogtooth Lake, which is marked by jack pine trees and gnarly granite hummocks rising out of the ground. You may notice that the pine trees on Dogtooth Lake are all the same height. This is no freak of nature. A forest fire in 1910 cracked open jack pine cones, which scattered heat-resistant seeds. The trees, of course, all took root at the same time.

Hikers on the scenic Lower Rapids Trail loop should keep

their eyes (and ears) peeled for the call of the green frog and the persistent singing of the red-eyed vireo. Songbirds, warblers, sparrows, blue herons and other vireos attract birders from all over, some of whom are fortunate enough to observe loons — a species that is experiencing habitat loss all over North America.

In the summer months, the interpretive centre staff organize wildlife presentations and talks about the wonders (animal, vegetable and mineral) of the boreal forest that dominates the park. Wintertime visitors can make use of the 16-kilometre network of groomed cross-country ski trails. Winter hiking and snowshoeing are also possible.

While many canoeists use Rushing River Provincial Park as a gateway to the stellar routes in Eagle-Dogtooth Provincial Park, there are plenty of wilderness canoe routes within Rushing River. They range from 30 to 100 kilometres in length, and novices will need to assess their ability to portage. One option is to start the 32-kilometre Dogtooth Lake–Little Dogtooth Lake route and reassess after the first short portage, which is 100 metres long, from Kilvert Lake to Swamp Lake. Also on the water, anglers fish for walleye, pike, smallmouth bass and lake trout. Visit the Rushing River General Store south of the park for a fishing licence.

Rushing River Provincial Park is ideally suited for beginner campers and nature enthusiasts as well as experienced backcountry paddlers. There are plenty of campsite options with electrical service (as well as rental RVs) so roughing it isn't necessary. You can also rent kayaks and canoes at the park office.

↑ **Visitors get excellent views of the fast-flowing Rushing River from the footbridge.**

↓ **Rushing River Provincial Park is home to a variety of songbirds, like the red-eyed vireo, which sings almost constantly.**

# Spruce Woods Provincial Park

*The presence of the northern prairie skink, Manitoba's only native lizard, can be surprising, but so too are the towering desert-like sand dunes*

## What Makes This Hot Spot Hot?

- The park is home to the Spirit Sands, the only set of sand dunes in all of Manitoba.
- A beautiful blue-green pond called the Devil's Punch Bowl was formed by underground streams eroding and collapsing the hills.
- Manitoba's only native lizard, the northern prairie skink, hangs out on the grassy hillsides.

**Address:** Provincial Trunk Hwy 5, 29 km south of the Trans-Canada Hwy (Hwy 1)
**GPS:** 49.66239; –99.26687
**Tel:** (1-888) 482-2267
**Website:** gov.mb.ca/sd/parks

**Open year-round**

🚶 🔭 🚴 🧗 ⚡ 🏊 ⛺

♿ **(Check ahead)**

You're ambling through Spruce Woods Provincial Park, and suddenly you come upon a stretch of 30-metre-high sand dunes, pincushion cacti and perhaps one or two hognose snakes. This is Manitoba? You walk another 30 minutes, and the vista changes again. Suddenly an oasis of spruce trees next to a blue-green spring-fed pond comes into view. Such are the contrasts of Spirit Sands and the Devil's Punch Bowl — two diverse habitats within Spruce Woods Provincial Park, 180 kilometres outside Winnipeg.

Spirit Sands is the name of the 4-square-kilometre tract of sand that's like no other landform in Manitoba. It's the only remaining unvegetated area of the Assiniboine Delta, which prompts people to call it a desert, though the area receives nearly twice the amount of precipitation than a true desert does. Back when ancient Lake Agassiz still existed (before it was drained thousands of years ago), the area was covered with 6,500 square kilometres of delta sand. Only these 4 square kilometres remain visible — the rest is now covered by plants and inhabited by wildlife.

A short distance away, the sand slides down a 45-metre depression into a pool of blue-green water known as the Devil's Punch Bowl, which is the result of underground streams eroding and collapsing the hills. Visitors to Spruce Woods Provincial Park can view these curiosities of nature by following the self-guided Spirit Sands/Devil's Punch Bowl Trail. The trail has boardwalks and stairs, so visitors can tour the area and

↗ **Spirit Sands, a 4-square-kilometre tract of sand, is like no other landform in Manitoba.**

minimize disturbance to the sand and vegetation.

Spruce Woods Provincial Park also encompasses spruce parkland (hence its name), upland deciduous forest and mixed-grass prairie within its 269 square kilometres. Wildlife varies depending on the section of the park. White-tailed deer make their home in the parkland, while ruffed grouse, raccoons and various species of weasels are drawn to the lush riverbanks. In spring and summer, you may spot a surprising species scuttling across the ground in Spruce Woods. The northern prairie skink, the only lizard native to Manitoba, is found in areas with sandy soil and mixed-grass prairie vegetation. The skink spends more than seven months of the year hibernating underground and requires the park's sandy soil for its winter burrow.

Nature lovers can bed down at Kiche Manitou campground (which has 200 campsites) or head to one of the five designated hike-in camping sites along the Epinette Creek Trails. (A note to campers: it is illegal to use or transport disease-carrying elm firewood.)

Friends of Spruce Woods Provincial Park operate the Spirit Sands Interpretive Centre and the Spirit Sands Museum. Volunteers lead interpretive tours throughout the summer. Other activities at the park include canoeing, swimming, hiking, horseback riding and biking. However, cyclists should note that, for environmental reasons, bikes are not allowed on the Spirit Sands/Devil's Punch Bowl, Isputinaw, Marsh Lake and Spring Ridge trails.

↑ Sand slides down a 45-metre depression into a pool of blue-green water known as the Devil's Punch Bowl.

↓ In spring and summer, the northern prairie skink is typically found in areas with sandy soil and mixed-grass prairie vegetation.

# Turtle Mountain Provincial Park

**Painted turtles, an abundance of shallow lakes and some of the largest oak trees in Manitoba**

## What Makes This Hot Spot Hot?

- The area has a high concentration of western painted turtles.
- There are more than 200 shallow lakes in the park, along with deciduous forests, marshland and undulating hills.
- The park is home to some of the largest oak trees in the province, survivors of turn-of-the-century forest fires.

**Address:** John Bracken Hwy (Provincial Trunk Hwy 10), about 100 km south of Brandon, MB
**GPS:** 49.04936; −100.06085
**Tel:** (1-800) 214-6497
**Website:** gov.mb.ca/sd/parks

**Open year-round**

↗ **Western painted turtles, the only subspecies of painted turtle found in Manitoba, are ubiquitous in the waters and wetlands of Turtle Mountain Provincial Park.**

As the name suggests, turtles — western painted turtles to be precise — thrive in Turtle Mountain Provincial Park, which comprises 184 square kilometres of shallow lakes, deciduous forests, marshland and undulating hills in the southwestern part of Manitoba. It's the numerous shallow lakes that account for the high concentration of western painted turtles — the only subspecies of painted turtle found in Manitoba — which thrive on the nutrient-rich water.

The western variety is the most brightly patterned of the four subspecies of painted turtles — recognized by their distinct olive-green and brown shells with touches of red and the bold yellow stripes on their heads and legs. Western painted turtles can be spotted basking near the edges of water bodies, typically on floating logs, rocks or small islands. If you visit the park in late spring and early summer, you might catch the females laying their eggs in sandy soil.

The shallow lakes and ponds are also natural landing spots for migrating waterfowl, which can be viewed in the fall. Salamanders, muskrats, beavers, raccoons, minks and moose also frequent these shallow water bodies. You might also spot deer and elk.

The park has some of the largest oak trees, the sole survivors of forest fires that swept through the region in the early 1900s. Interpretive maps, which outline trails and wildlife habitats, can be picked up at the Adam Lake Campground Office. The Wildlife Self-Guided Trail passes by an area favoured by beavers, where their dams, mounds of surreptitiously placed logs and branches rising above the water, are fairly easy to spot. Turtle's Back Trail, which starts at William Lake, climbs 66 metres and leads to a lookout tower that gives you breathtaking views of the park. Other diversions within the park include camping, swimming, fishing and biking (especially mountain biking).

↑ Your best bet for spotting an industrious beaver is to hike along the Wildlife Self-Guided Trail, which passes by a number of beaver dams.

↖ With over 200 lakes, water figures prominently in Turtle Mountain Provincial Park, which is known for family-friendly camping and plenty of recreational activities.

# Whiteshell Provincial Park

**This 2,721-square-kilometre park is home to Manitoba's deepest lake, a glacially carved pond that gets covered over with lilies each summer, and a world-class goose sanctuary**

## What Makes This Hot Spot Hot?

- With Canadian Shield, boreal forests, sandy beaches, rock ridges and bogs, there's no shortage of protected parkland to explore.
- West Hawk Lake, Manitoba's deepest lake, is popular with scuba divers.
- Each fall, over 1,000 Canada geese prepare for fall migration at the Alfred Hole Goose Sanctuary.

**Address:** 130 km east of Winnipeg, MB; follow the Trans-Canada Hwy (Hwy 1) or Provincial Trunk Hwy 44
**GPS:** 49.74585; −95.21349
**Tel:** (1-866) 626-4862
**Website:** whiteshell.mb.ca

**Open year-round; Alfred Hole's visitor centre is open May until Thanksgiving**

&#9855; (Limited, check ahead)

Located close to the Manitoba-Ontario border, Whiteshell Provincial Park comprises 2,721 square kilometres of protected wilderness parkland, which includes about 200 lakes, rushing rivers, rugged Canadian Shield, boreal forests, ancient rock ridges, sandy beaches and bogs.

A crashing meteorite gets the credit for creating one of the more surprising visitor activities in Whiteshell Provincial Park: scuba diving at West Hawk Lake. The impact of the meteorite on the ancient, mostly granite rock bed resulted in the deepest lake in Manitoba, reaching a depth of 115 metres. Geologists estimate that the crater at the bottom of the lake could be 100 million years old.

Hundreds of kilometres of trails cater to hikers (and, in the winter, skiers and snowshoers) of all levels. Experienced hikers gravitate to the Mantario Trail, a 60-kilometre hike (which takes three to six days) through Canadian Shield. Paddlers have 325 kilometres of canoe routes to explore. The 170-kilometre Caddy Lake Canoe Route takes canoeists through rock tunnels blasted out of granite during railroad construction in the early 1900s.

Legions of plant lovers visit Lily Pond (on Highway 44, west of Caddy Lake) during the summer months when the pond is blanketed with white and yellow lilies. The towering bedrock cliffs surrounding Lily Pond are popular with rock climbers.

There's plenty of wildlife to spot, some more elusive than others: wolves, white-tailed deer, moose, turkey vultures and otters, to name a handful. Black bears inhabit the park, which means visitors must adhere to Bear Smart safety guidelines. There's also no shortage of species to draw birdwatchers year-round. Chickadees, grey and blue jays, pine and evening grosbeaks, redpolls, woodpeckers and owls are all found here, even in the cold months. Bald eagles and ruby-throated hummingbirds make appearances in summer. An annual event that really pulls in bird lovers is the

migration of over 1,000 Canada geese from the Alfred Hole Goose Sanctuary.

Petroforms, sometimes called boulder mosaics, are found at various sites throughout the park, such as Bannock Point. Anishinaabe and other Indigenous Peoples believe that thousands of years ago the rocks were laid out on the bedrock in the shapes of humans, fish, snakes and turtles as part of teaching and healing ceremonies. These rock formations are known to the Anishinaabe as *manitouabee*, meaning "where the spirit sits."

## Alfred Hole Goose Sanctuary

It's a tale that many people remember for its feel-good, Disney-like beginning, but it's very much a story about wildlife and nature conservation.

One day in the spring of 1939, mink rancher Alfred Hole rescued four baby goslings on his property near Rennie, about a 2-hour drive east of Winnipeg. The goslings were members of our national bird family — *Branta canadensis*, or the Canada goose.

Unfazed at the prospect of raising geese, the mink rancher housed the goslings in

↑ **West Hawk Lake, in the heart of Whiteshell Provincial Park, is the deepest lake in Manitoba, reaching a depth of 115 metres in places.**

↓ **Petroforms are rock formations in the shapes of humans, fish, snakes, turtles and other animals. For the Anishinaabe, these ancient rock formations are important, sacred sites.**

↑ Hundreds of Canada geese return to Alfred Hole Goose Sanctuary in Rennie each spring to hatch their goslings.

↗ Late August to October is the best time to visit Alfred Hole to observe the iconic V-shaped flying formation.

→ Many Canada geese return to Alfred Hole each spring to hatch new generations of goslings.

a pen, fed them dandelions and gave them full run of his pond, which they eventually shared with other wildlife. Later that season Hole acquired a gander, which mated with one of the females, and soon after more eggs were laid and hatched. Come autumn, the geese responded to the instinctive call of nature and joined the annual fall migration southward, and they returned the following spring.

By the time Hole died in 1959, he had established — with the support of private groups, individuals and the Ministry of Natural Resources — a full-fledged goose sanctuary that's become one of the key attractions at Whiteshell

Provincial Park. Currently, hundreds of Canada Geese return each spring to the Alfred Hole Goose Sanctuary to hatch their goslings.

The best times to go? The ideal time to admire baby goslings is mid-May to July. To observe the iconic V-shaped flying formation as the geese head south, visit late August to October.

Take the self-guided Alfred Hole Goose Sanctuary Trail to observe the fauna and flora attracted to the pond. During the summer months, staff at the interpretive centre can teach you about the history of the Canada goose, the aerodynamics of their V-formation and their social habits.

# Central Manitoba and Opasquia

# Bakers Narrows Provincial Park

## *Canadian Shield, boreal forest and one of Manitoba's top fishing lakes*

### What Makes This Hot Spot Hot?

- A viewing tower lets visitors look out over the park's 145 hectares of boreal forest.
- Lake Athapapuskow is respected by anglers worldwide for trophy sport fishing.
- Swimming and boating opportunities abound on the shores of Lake Athapapuskow.

**Address:** Provincial Trunk Hwy 10, 19 km southeast of Flin Flon, MB
**GPS:** 54.67505; −101.66304
**Tel:** (1-888) 482-2267
**Website:** gov.mb.ca/sd/parks

**Open May to September**

🚶 🔭 ⚲ ⚑ 🚣 🏊 ⛺

♿ (Check ahead)

↗ **Dominating the view from above, Lake Athapapuskow is world-renowned for the trophy rainbow trout, walleye and perch fished from its waters.**

If you only do one thing at Bakers Narrows Provincial Park, make sure it's a visit to the viewing tower, which rewards visitors with spectacular views of the surrounding forests, rocks and lake. From the tower you can look out over the park's 145 hectares of boreal forest, featuring both coniferous and deciduous tree species — black spruce, jack pine, white spruce and trembling aspen — that are sturdy enough to thrive on the Canadian Shield.

The other perk for anyone who climbs the viewing tower? Park staff have installed five interpretive signs at the top that chronicle the area's rich fur-trading history.

The glacial lake that dominates the view is Lake Athapapuskow — Cree for "rocks all around" — which comprises three connected water bodies: Big Athapap to the south, Little Athapap in the middle and the North Arm. Bakers Narrows Provincial Park is located at the narrows between the North Arm and Little Athapap.

Lake Athapapuskow is considered one of the best fishing lakes in Canada. World-renowned for the size of its rainbow trout, walleye and perch, the lake is a huge draw for anglers, who also come for its northern pike, lake trout, lake whitefish, burbot, white sucker, tullibee, splake and smallmouth bass.

There are other ways to enjoy the area's fantastic waters. Two family-friendly beaches on the shores of Lake Athapapuskow are perfect for those who love to be in the water, and several docks and boat launches are great for those who prefer to glide on it. The provincial park also features electrical and basic campsites as well as six yurts, which include wheelchair-accessible and pet-friendly yurts.

→ **The viewing tower provides the perfect setting for nature lovers: panoramas of the park's 145 hectares of boreal forest.**

# Clearwater Lake Provincial Park

*Caves, a glacial moraine and some of the deepest (and coldest) waters in Manitoba*

## What Makes This Hot Spot Hot?

- The uncommonly deep Clearwater Lake is 16 kilometres in diameter, taking up almost half the park.
- Visitors can explore dolomite caves that have formed on the shores of Clearwater Lake.
- To the south, visitors can spot the Cusp of The Pas Moraine, one of the most prominent geological formations in Manitoba.

**Address:** Provincial Rd 287, 18 km north of The Pas, MB
**GPS:** 53.99664; –100.95032
**Tel:** (1-888) 482-2267
**Website:** gov.mb.ca/sd/parks

**Open year-round**

&#9855; (Check ahead)

In 2017, Manitobans voted Clearwater Lake the best provincial park in the province — largely because of the lake itself, which takes up almost half of the 593-square-kilometre park.

Clearwater Lake is renowned for its excellent water quality and large lake trout, which thrive in its deep, cool, clear waters, luring anglers from far and wide. The crystalline, circular lake has an average depth of 13.1 metres but gets as deep as 39 metres in places. The reason for such clear water? The lake is spring-fed, which means the amount of sediment is minimal compared with lakes fed by rivers and streams.

Many hikers and budding geologists visit Clearwater

Lake Provincial Park to hike the Caves Self-Guiding Trail. "The Caves" are deep crevices that were formed when rock masses separated from the shoreline cliffs, leaving cave-like spaces and vertical fractures between layers of dolomite bedrock. Park staff have built stairways and viewing platforms along the designated trail, and they're quick to warn you to stay on the path, both for your own safety and also to protect the sensitive plant life in the area. Wildlife, such as black bears, squirrels and weasels, use the cave-like spaces for shelter.

In addition to fishing, other diversions include swimming, boating, hiking and camping. In the winter, park staff maintain a day-use area east of Pioneer Bay for visitors to enjoy cross-country skiing, skating and tobogganing.

Clearwater Lake is a few kilometres south of another interesting geological feature: the Cusp of The Pas Moraine, a crescent-like escarpment formed during the last ice age. The Pas Moraine, which is 16 kilometres wide, rises 60 metres above the surrounding terrain, making it one of the most prominent glacial formations in central Manitoba.

↑ **The crystalline Clearwater Lake takes up almost half of the 593-square-kilometre park.**

← **The clear quality of the lake's water is due to the fact that it's spring-fed and doesn't contain the sediment that is typically carried into river-fed lakes.**

↓ **"The Caves" are deep crevices that were formed when rock masses separated from the shoreline cliffs.**

# Little Limestone Lake Provincial Park

**A touch of the Caribbean in Manitoba thanks to a huge marl lake that changes colour throughout the day**

## What Makes This Hot Spot Hot?

- At 4,000 hectares, Little Limestone Lake is the largest marl lake in the world.
- Limestone cliffs provide excellent winter habitats for bats.
- This park is the only area in Manitoba where four of the province's hoofed creatures share the same habitat.

**Address:** Provincial Trunk Hwy 6, about 60 km north of Grand Rapids, MB
**GPS:** 53.74223; −99.32264
**Tel:** (1-888) 482-2267
**Website:** gov.mb.ca/sd/parks

**Open year-round; park is non-operational with no facilities**

↗ **Little brown bats find hibernacula, or winter habitats, in the park's limestone cliffs, which offer protection from predators.**

L ittle Limestone Lake Provincial Park, sometimes called "Manitoba's Caribbean" because of the lake's water colour, is a protected area — and for a very good reason: it's the world's largest and most outstanding marl lake. It's also known as Manitoba's "Colour-Changing Lake."

A marl lake changes colour as the temperature of the water rises in summer, causing the calcite in the water to separate and form tiny crystals. This turns the water from clear to an opaque turquoise colour, surprisingly similar to the waters of the Caribbean. Many visitors have watched this lake's water change from a brilliant turquoise in the morning to a robin's egg blue by the afternoon.

This area is a distinct natural space for another reason: little brown bats (*Myotis lucifugus*) have discovered excellent winter habitats in caves carved out of the

region's limestone cliffs.

The park is home to an array of species, including songbirds, waterfowl, moose, muskrats, eagles, lynx, foxes and woodland caribou. According to wildlife experts, it also has the distinction of being the only area in Manitoba where four of the province's hoofed animal species are found living in the same habitat: deer, wood bison, elk and moose. Birders

typically spot ring-billed gulls, double-crested cormorants, common terns and various species of ducks and geese, all of which inhabit the lake and shoreline.

The area around the shoreline of Little Limestone Lake is protected, meaning visitors cannot do anything that impacts the environment or the area's wildlife. The park itself is non-operational, so there are no camping facilities, boat access sites, roads or marked trails.

↑ **Sometimes referred to as Manitoba's "Colour-Changing Lake," Little Limestone Lake is the largest marl lake in the world.**

→ **The common tern is one of numerous bird species regularly sighted in the park.**

NORTHWESTERN ONTARIO

# Opasquia Provincial Park

*An epic adventure through the gathering place of the Gulo gulo, the scientific name for the wolverine*

## What Makes This Hot Spot Hot?

- Opasquia provides denning habitat for a large population of wolverines.
- The park encompasses distinctive geology, like the 2-kilometre-wide Opasquia Moraine.
- The area is abundant in wildlife, with everything from bears and beavers to walleye and whitefish.

**Address:** There is no direct road access into the park. To fly in, make arrangements with outfitters in Bissett or Matheson Island, MB, or in Red Lake or Pickle Lake, ON
**GPS:** 53.52263; −93.06887
**Tel:** (1-807) 727-1336
**Website:** ontarioparks.com

**Open year-round; park is non-operational with no facilities**

↗ **This expanse of undisturbed wilderness is a perfect home for a variety of wildlife, including the beavers that constructed this enormous dam.**

Opasquia Provincial Park, close to the Manitoba-Ontario border, has an interesting mix of natural attributes to pique the curiosity of visitors: an abundance of wolverines, a 2-kilometre-wide moraine and plenty of fish.

And then there's the solitude, part of any journey into a 473,000-hectare wilderness area. Opasquia Provincial Park is accessible only by float plane, which means it never gets crowded — far from it.

The nearest city is Red Lake, Ontario, which is 250 kilometres away.

The park's distinctive geology is key to why it's protected: Opasquia Moraine, a 2-kilometre-wide glacial till, rises 100 metres above the surrounding land. The moraine marks what was once the limit of the ancient glacial Lake Agassiz. The landscape is now covered in thick forests of mostly spruce, along with poplar, tamarack, birch and ash.

Opasquia provides denning habitat for a large population of wolverines. There are other animals in this wilderness region: moose, bears, eagles, otters, beavers and wolves. Fish species include northern pike, walleye, whitefish and perch, so consequently fishing opportunities are abundant here. Whitewater canoeing and wilderness trekking are the other primary activities in this remote paradise. Note: there are no designated trails.

Opasquia Provincial Park is a protected wilderness park that is non-operational, meaning there are no facilities such as campgrounds or support services. With no established campsites, campers are urged to set up in cleared areas and "leave nothing but footprints," taking out everything they bring in. As there are no roads into the park, to visit you must arrange float plane services. Outfitters based in Bissett and Matheson Island in Manitoba or Pickle Lake and Red Lake in Ontario fly into Opasquia.

↑ Dozens of rivers flow through Opasquia Provincial Park, making it appealing to experienced paddlers.

↓ Wolverines require snow for denning purposes, which partly explains why they're so abundant in this region.

# Wekusko Falls Provincial Park

*Abundant nature, incredible canoeing and a rushing waterfall*

## What Makes This Hot Spot Hot?

- A loop trail and two suspension bridges allow visitors to get close to the roaring Wekusko Falls.
- There are numerous canoe routes through the park that enable paddlers to navigate a variety of lakes and rivers.
- The nearby Tramping Lake pictographs are among the province's finest rock paintings.

**Address:** Provincial Rd 392, 15 km south of Snow Lake, MB
**GPS:** 54.79378; −99.97509
**Tel:** (1-888) 482-2267
**Website:** gov.mb.ca/sd/parks

**Open May long weekend to Labour Day**

&#9927; (Check ahead)

↗ **Hikers get a true sense of the force of the Grass River while crossing one of two suspension bridges over the plunging Wekusko Falls.**

The Grass River plunges almost 12 metres down a series of falls and rapids known as Wekusko Falls. There's a suspension bridge close to the provincial park's campground that allows you to get close to the falls as well as a footbridge that crosses directly over a set of rapids as the river rolls into Wekusko Lake.

The Grass River offers canoeists numerous options for exploring different areas of the park (and far beyond). Adventurous paddlers who are keen to tackle the entire 724-kilometre Grass River will pass through a series of lakes and rivers and should be prepared to portage.

Many opt to follow the 190-kilometre route from Cranberry Portage to Wekusko Lake. Along the way, canoeists can see the Tramping Lake rock paintings (viewable only by boat), which are estimated to be between 1,500 and 3,000 years old. The pictographs, depicting wildlife and Indigenous customs, were painted on a vertical

rock surface 7 kilometres south-west of Wekusko Falls.

Visitors will find balsam and other conifers growing in the mixed-wood boreal forests. Plant lovers have spotted the calypso orchid (also called the fairy slipper or Venus's slipper), which thrives in the shade of the boreal forest.

There are basic camping facilities as well as a few lodges, which attract campers, canoeists and anglers who come to fish for giant northern pike, lake trout and walleye.

↑ There's an abundance of calm lakes and rushing rivers for paddlers of every skill level.

→ The park's campground is within walking (and hearing) distance of the falls.

NUNAVUT

Hudson Bay

Seal R.

Churchill

Churchhill R.

Little Churchill R.

Nelson R.

Amery

Split
Lake

Gillam

391

280

Nelson
House

Thompson

Nelson R.

6

Hayes R.

Gods R.

# Northern Manitoba

# Caribou River Provincial Wilderness Park

*This wilderness park, on the southern border of Nunavut, protects the fall and winter ranges of the Qamanirjuaq herd of barren-ground caribou*

## What Makes This Hot Spot Hot?

- The park contains caribou calving grounds and is the winter home for the threatened barren-ground caribou.
- The rapids of the Caribou River are great for paddling.
- Glacier-carved landforms, forests, rocky outcrops and rivers define the rugged landscape.

**Address:** There is no direct road access into the park. To fly in, make arrangements with outfitters or air charter companies in Churchill, MB, that service the park
**GPS:** 59.48736; −96.65341
**Tel:** (1-800) 214-6497
**Website:** gov.mb.ca/sd/parks

**Open year-round; park is non-operational with no facilities**

In a remote area this vast and seldom visited, who pays attention to borders? The 7,640-square-kilometre Caribou River Provincial Wilderness Park is the most northerly provincial park in Manitoba, situated below the border of Nunavut. The area continues to be used by the Sayisi Dene First Nation and Inuit of the Kivalliq region of Nunavut.

The park protects an area of the Taiga Shield ecozone. The terrain is made up of boreal forests, rivers, lakes, bogs, marshes, glacier-carved ridges (such as eskers) and rocky outcrops. The Caribou River is known for its pristine rapids, making it appealing to experienced long-distance canoeists. This land is uninhabitable for most creatures, as permafrost severely limits the growth of trees, but it's a paradise of sorts for barren-ground caribou.

The park protects the fall and winter ranges of the migratory Qamanirjuaq barren-ground caribou herd. (There are about a dozen herds of barren-ground caribou in North America.) The Qamanirjuaq herd can be found primarily in Manitoba and Nunavut, with portions of

the herd found in southeastern parts of the Northwest Territories and northeastern parts of Saskatchewan. Since 1995, when the park opened, this area has provided the caribou with calving grounds and a safe place to spend the winter.

In late 2016, barren-ground caribou were classified as "threatened" by the Committee on the Status of Endangered Wildlife in Canada. By 2018, barren-ground caribou were added to the list of "species at risk" in the Northwest Territories.

Most visitors arrive by plane, which means you might catch some incredible in-flight entertainment: a bird's-eye view of migrating barren-ground caribou down below. Whether going for hunting, fishing or canoeing, or just admiring the caribou, you must plan your excursion in advance. Canoeists are advised to check seasonal water levels with park officials before flying in. The park accommodates only wilderness camping since there are no dedicated campgrounds. Visitors are expected to set up camp only on sites that look to be previously used, often marked by a firepit.

↑ The park protects the fall and winter ranges of the migratory Qamanirjuaq barren-ground caribou herd.

↖ The Caribou River is popular with seasoned long-distance canoeists.

# Churchill

***Known as the "Polar Bear Capital of the World," Churchill is the go-to destination not just for polar bear viewing but also to see beloved belugas and the northern lights***

## What Makes This Hot Spot Hot?

- Churchill is the most popular human settlement in the world where visitors can view the majestic polar bear up close.
- About 60,000 beluga whales congregate along the Hudson Bay coast from June to September.
- Churchill's position directly beneath the northern hemisphere's auroral oval makes it one of the best locations on the planet to witness the northern lights.

**Address:** There is no direct road access into Churchill. Flights from Winnipeg via Gimli are popular. Trains are available between Winnipeg and Churchill
**GPS:** 58.76841; −94.16496
**Tel:** (1-800) 665-0040
**Website:** everythingchurchill.com

**Open year-round**

&#9855; **(Limited, check ahead)**

Mention "Churchill" to a nature lover, and you'll get at least one of three responses: polar bears, beluga whales or the northern lights.

While polar bears put Churchill on the map (it's recognized as the "Polar Bear Capital of the World"), most people visit this region on the southern edge of Canada's arctic to fulfill a bucket-list dream that also includes up-close encounters with beluga whales and witnessing aurora borealis. The time of year you decide to visit will likely be dictated by the species or natural phenomena you wish to observe.

Churchill, long categorized as "the accessible arctic," is home to wildlife species that are native to three distinct ecozones: arctic marine, arctic tundra and boreal forest.

Three options are available to observe the polar bears: safely seated in tundra buggies, eye-to-eye through strong buffalo fences that surround a handful of northern lodges or on foot with an expert guide on a walking safari. The prime viewing times are in October and November, when the polar bears travel from their summer habitat on the tundra back to their ice-and-snow-covered seal-hunting territory on the Hudson Bay. However, many bears come as early as July.

Then there are other wildlife enthusiasts who are besotted with the beluga whales, which have been called "sea canaries" because of their singular high-pitched whistles, chirps, clicks and eerie calls from below the water. From June to September, about 60,000 belugas (the largest concentration of the species in the world) take over the waters off the Hudson Bay coastline, where they seem comfortable with the kayaks, Zodiacs and tour boats that enable visitors to watch the belugas (some of them 3 to 4 metres in length) frolic in the water.

The region has lots of other flora and fauna to discover — arctic foxes, red foxes, moose, black bears, caribou, wolves, seals, 250 species of birds (migratory and shorebirds) and more than 400 native plant species, including scarlet bearberries, yellow willows and white mountain avens — as well as one of the planet's greatest celestial spectacles.

Do the northern lights — that colourful, sweeping, dancing explosion of light in the northern night sky — actually make a sound? It's an oft-debated discussion among night-sky watchers. Some claim there's a

swishing sound while others talk about a crackling noise when the lights appear. What is 100 per cent certain, however, is the astounding beauty of this phenomenon, which occurs when charged particles from the sun become trapped in the earth's magnetic field, resulting

↑ Visitors on-board a tundra buggy can safely encounter polar bears in their natural setting.

↖ The Churchill region is one of the biggest polar bear denning areas in the world, so mothers and cubs are frequently spotted.

in a vibrant display of greens, purples, reds and yellows across the dark northern skies. The best times to view aurora borealis? On a clear night between January and March and from late August to early September. (The aurora is typically not visible during May, June and July, when the nighttime skies tend to be bright.)

Nature enthusiasts can sign up for courses at the Churchill Northern Studies Centre, an independent, not-for-profit research and education facility that offers a range of educational programming for students and visiting researchers. The centre, which also provides accommodation, is located 23 kilometres east of town.

After an extended disruption in rail service to Churchill, the Hudson Bay Railway was on track for repair as this book was going to press. Starting in spring 2019, nature lovers should be able to travel from Winnipeg to Churchill by rail, though travellers should check ahead before booking tours and accommodations.

↑ About 60,000 belugas (the largest concentration of the whales in the world) take over the waters off the Hudson Bay coastline from June to September.

↖ The red fox is one of many wildlife species that call the Churchill area home.

← Mountain white avens add a splash of colour to the arctic landscape.

→ The optimal time to see the northern lights is on a clear night between January and March or between late August and early September.

includes moose, black bears, timber wolves, arctic foxes, wolverines and snowshoe hares. Pine grosbeaks, tree sparrows, Harris's sparrows and grey-cheeked thrushes are among the common bird species found here.

Numaykoos Lake Provincial Park is also known for its frost polygons, which are unique geometric patterns on the ground formed by the repeated seasonal freezing and thawing of the soil. Visible ice wedges gradually take shape on the frozen tundra. But don't go looking for them on foot — they're only visible from the air.

The forests are thin and trees are generally shorter in this region, which is part of the subarctic zone. Much of the soil is perennially frozen.

There are no designated campsites in the 3,600-square-kilometre park. Visitors are urged to camp in spots that look to have been used previously, rather than setting up on unblemished terrain. The park is not accessible by road, so to reach it you must arrange flights with outfitters or air charter companies that service northern Manitoba.

⬆ The snowshoe hare, one of the wildlife species frequently spotted in Numaykoos Lake Provincial Park, can travel up to 45 kilometres per hour.

⬉ Barren-ground caribou migrate southwards from the Northwest Territories and spend the winters in this largely undisturbed park.

# Pisew Falls Provincial Park

*The best place in the province to chase waterfalls is in remote northeastern Manitoba*

## What Makes This Hot Spot Hot?

- A hiking trail takes visitors from the second-highest waterfalls in Manitoba (Pisew Falls) to the highest (Kwasitchewan Falls).
- There are basic backcountry campsites near Kwasitchewan Falls for those wishing to camp overnight.
- The ever-present mist from the waterfalls creates a microclimate that encourages the growth of mosses, lichens and fungi.

**Address:** Provincial Trunk Hwy 6, 74 km south of Thompson, MB
**GPS:** 55.19849; −98.39783
**Tel:** (204) 677-6648
**Website:** gov.mb.ca/sd/parks

**Open year-round**

&#9855; (Limited, check ahead)

↗ **The ice build-up at Pisew Falls in winter creates a dramatic winter shot.**

The Cree, one of the largest First Nations groups in North America, named this provincial park's falls *Pisew*, which means "lynx," not because the animal roamed the region but because the hissing sound of the water is similar to that of the wild feline.

Visitors to Pisew Falls Provincial Park, many of whom travel 700 kilometres from Winnipeg, are rewarded with views of the two highest waterfalls in the province. Standing at 13 metres tall and a short walk away from the parking lot, Pisew Falls is easy to access and admire — there is a viewing platform as well as a bridge below the falls that crosses the Grass River. Downriver, the 14-metre-high Kwasitchewan Falls beats Pisew Falls by a mere metre, making it the highest in the province. Enthusiasts who are keen to check out both waterfalls can take the 22-kilometre return hike known as the Upper Track Trail, which mostly follows the Grass River from Pisew Falls to Kwasitchewan Falls. This adventure is ideal for overnight campers who want to sleep outdoors for just one night. Upriver from Kwasitchewan Falls, there are backcountry

⬆ Pisew Falls, at 13 metres, is the second-highest waterfall in Manitoba.

campsites with basic toilet facilities so that visitors don't contaminate the water. Note that this is a pack in–pack out site and that camping right at the falls is forbidden.

Black bears have been noted in the area (hikers report sightings of bear scat), so all visitors are encouraged to practice Bear Smart outdoor guidelines. Otters frequent the waterfalls year-round, and bald eagles have been spotted nesting in the tamarack trees.

The microclimate created by the near-constant mist in the vicinity of Pisew Falls has resulted in the growth of mosses, lichens and fungi. Botanists have also found various ferns near the falls that apparently date back to the ice age. Consequently, the area immediately surrounding the falls is deemed "environ-mentally sensitive," so be sure to stick to the designated observation platforms and trails when viewing the falls. The mist also makes the area slippery year-round, especially in the winter when it ices over. Pisew Falls can be visited in the cold months, but extreme caution is advised as snow and ice near the falls can make conditions dangerous.

# Wapusk National Park

*The home of about 1,000 polar bears and the stomping grounds for a herd of 3,000 caribou*

## What Makes This Hot Spot Hot?

- Wapusk National Park is one of the largest polar bear denning areas in the world.
- The 3,000-strong Cape Churchill caribou herd roams the park and can be viewed from a small aircraft.
- The park is home to many other unique animals, including 250 species of birds.

**Address:** There is no direct road access into the park. Visitors fly in to either Churchill or Gillam and then travel into the park by boat, snowmobile, aircraft or dogsled
**GPS:** 57.79385; −93.22902
**Tel:** (1-888) 773-8888
**Website:** pc.gc.ca/en/pn-np

**Open year-round**

↗ **Wapusk National Park is one of the largest polar bear denning areas in the world.**

apusk is the Cree word for "white bear." This name, especially when spoken aloud, has a mystical quality about it, which is rivalled only by the magic of observing a polar bear in its natural setting for the first time. And that's the main reason visitors make the trek to this expansive park in the remote subarctic. Wapusk National Park encompasses a large portion of the Hudson and James Bay Lowlands, where the terrain is a mix of boreal forest, arctic tundra, muskeg and expansive peat bogs that make up one of the largest polar bear denning areas in the world.

Visitors to the park are, without fail, rendered awestruck on their first sighting of a polar bear in the wild. The average adult male weighs between 300 and 450 kilograms, though wildlife experts have recorded one beast that weighed more than 700 kilograms. To spot a polar bear on ice is one visitor experience, but, depending on the season, there are opportunities to catch mama bears and playful cubs frolicking on the tundra. Female polar bears give birth every two or three years. While moms are frequently observed with two cubs, it's not uncommon to see triplets. But don't ever get close, and heading out alone (whether hiking or camping) is strongly discouraged.

Seasoned outfitters, most of

which are based in Churchill, or Parks Canada guides welcome nature lovers at different times of the year. February is prime season to see polar bears on the ice. March is typically when mothers and newborn cubs leave their dens and play in the snow for the first time. Many polar bears migrate along the coast from late September to November to catch the first pack ice of the winter, where they'll feed on seals before returning to land, fatted from their feasting.

Most visitors get to experience polar bears from the safety of a tundra buggy, an elevated vehicle (beyond the reach of the bears) that traverses tundra, snow and ice. There are also on-foot "safaris," typically in the fall. On these treks, visitors are accompanied by guides with tranquilizer guns. Safety — for both bears and humans — is paramount during any excursion.

In addition to bears, there are plenty of other wildlife viewing opportunities in Wapusk National Park: arctic foxes, arctic hares, wolves and wolverines as well as more than 250 bird species. Winged species include Caspian terns, great grey owls, sandhill cranes, stilt sandpipers, Hudsonian godwits, Ross's and ivory gulls, snow geese, Canada geese, arctic loons, peregrine falcons and gyrfalcons (the largest of the falcon family). And, of course,

there's the large Cape Churchill barren-ground caribou herd, which numbers around 3,000 and is best viewed on an aerial tour. The caribou roam the park year-round, wintering in the peatlands for warmth and moving to the Hudson Bay shoreline in summer. The herd calves in the northeastern corner of the park each spring.

In terms of other viewing opportunities, there are the stunning northern lights. Clear night skies from January to March and in late summer are optimal times to view nature's spectacular light display.

Visiting Wapusk National Park by water is another option. Experienced canoeists should consult Parks Canada when planning to undertake the 168-kilometre route along the Owl River, which crosses the entire park and takes four to seven days to complete. Canoe excursions are now restricted to June to avoid encounters with polar bears.

↑ The 11,475-square-kilometre Wapusk National Park encompasses a large portion of the Hudson and James Bay Lowlands.

↖ A herd of 3,000 barren-ground caribou, known as the Cape Churchill herd, roams the park.

# Special Interest

# Birdwatching

↑ **The dainty Tennessee warbler, known for its surprisingly loud staccato song, is frequently spotted in the Delta Marsh during spring and fall migrations.**

Manitoba lies within three migration corridors, so it's no surprise that over 390 species of birds have been sighted in the province. The combination of diverse habitats — grasslands, wetlands, boreal forest and subarctic — appeals to a huge array of winged creatures. Consequently, there's a well-established "birding infrastructure" in Manitoba in the form of birding trails, viewing mounds and sanctuaries. Manitoba's 500-kilometre **Pine to Prairie International Birding Trail** (page 34) draws birdwatchers from around the world, as does the **Alfred Hole Goose Sanctuary** in **Whiteshell Provincial Park** (page 49), where visitors get to witness migrating Canada geese and their iconic V-shaped flying formation across the fall sky. More than 300 species of birds have been sighted at **Oak Hammock Marsh** (page 26), where an estimated 100,000 waterfowl stop during their annual migration. The vast **Riding Mountain National Park** (page 36) is home to an estimated 250 species of birds, including the loon, the trumpeter swan and the golden-winged warbler, a rare sight in the province.

Manitoba also resonates with birders who have their favourites: songbirds, for instance, are among the sought-after species in **Birds Hill Provincial Park** (page 14) and **Duck Mountain Provincial Park** (page 16).

Here are some other nature hot spots popular with birding enthusiasts.

## Delta Marsh Wildlife Management Area

The Delta Marsh is one of the busiest bird monitoring stations in North America, largely due to the 7,500 migrating songbirds that pass through this wetland, situated at the south end of Lake Manitoba (about 25 kilometres north of Portage la Prairie). The 18,000-hectare Delta Marsh (always popular with waterfowl) is one of the largest freshwater coastal wetlands in Canada, stretching about 30 kilometres from St. Ambroise in the east to Lynch's Point in the west. Frequently sighted bird species, especially during spring and fall migrations, include yellow warblers, Tennessee warblers and myrtle warblers, followed by least flycatchers, song sparrows, American redstarts, northern waterthrush and white-throated sparrows.

The University of Manitoba operates the Delta Marsh Field

↑ Sunset goose flights attract birders to FortWhyte each fall. Flocks of geese start landing en masse about half an hour after the sun goes down.

Station, and the Delta Waterfowl Foundation oversees the Delta Waterfowl and Wetlands Research Station.

## FortWhyte Alive

FortWhyte Alive, in southwest Winnipeg, is an environmental, educational and recreational centre that sits along Manitoba's Pine to Prairie International Birding Trail. While birds are not the main draw to FortWhyte, the centre is high

↑ **The chestnut-collared longspur is a threatened grassland species that can be spotted along the Manitoba Grasslands Birding Trail. A ground-feeding bird, it's typically seen in areas with taller, denser grass.**

on the list for birders during spring (April and May) and fall (August and September) migrations. At least 160 year-round species of birds have been recorded at FortWhyte, drawn by the range of habitats — aspen forest, grassland, willow swamp, cattail marsh and sheltered lakes. Among the species making appearances at FortWhyte are bald eagles, golden eagles, ospreys, northern harriers, Cooper's hawks, northern goshawks, red-tailed hawks, eastern screech owls and great horned owls, to name a few. Those making

winter appearances include the pileated woodpecker, dark-eyed junco, common redpoll, white-breasted nuthatch and pine siskin.

Fall is especially popular with bird enthusiasts who want to experience the sunset goose flights. Throngs of birders arrive at FortWhyte just before sunset to watch the flocks of geese that start landing en masse about half an hour after the sun goes down. It's one of Mother Nature's most "Insta-grammable" moments, if you can get enough light!

## Manitoba Grasslands Birding Trail

The Manitoba Grasslands Birding Trail, in the south-western part of the province, is ideal for birders hoping to see some of the threatened and seldom-seen species of grassland birds, such as the burrowing owl, chestnut-collared longspur, Baird's sparrow, loggerhead shrike, ferruginous hawk and Sprague's pipit. The self-guided driving trail begins at the Gerald W. Malaher Wildlife Management Area, just west of the town of Melita. From there you can explore the 53-kilometre Northern Loop or the 127-kilometre Southern Loop. Both pass through a mix of habitats — mixed-grass prairies, wetlands, stands of willow, aspen and prairie shrubs, lush valleys, and dry ridges — that attract a variety of birds.

Visitors can pick up pamphlets (with route directions) at various businesses in Melita or online at gov.mb.ca.

## Whitewater Lake Wildlife Management Area

Whitewater Lake in south-western Manitoba, situated between Deloraine and Boissevain, is more of a marsh. The 8,260-hectare wildlife management area — where visitors will find a lookout tower, viewing mound, board-walk, trails and interpretive

signage — is a birder's paradise. Thousands of migrating tundra swans arrive in April-May and October-November. There are also an abundance of black-crowned night herons, snow geese, Franklin's gulls, mallards and pintails. The shallow saline wetland, sedge meadows and mixed-grass prairie provide food and nesting habitats not just for tundra swans but also for egrets, white-faced ibises, American avocets, Wilson's phalaropes and a variety of other shore-birds and waterfowl. Whitewater Lake also draws visitors from nearby Turtle Mountain Provincial Park.

↑ Franklin's gulls make their homes in floating nests made of bulrushes, cattails and, sometimes, material from neighbouring nests.

↑↑ An American avocet nests and feeds in the shallow wetlands at Whitewater Lake.

# Hiking

↑ History buffs and nature lovers are drawn to the 8.9-kilometre Grey Owl Trail, which leads to Grey Owl's cabin, the onetime home of Parks Canada's first resident naturalist.

Hiking opportunities in Manitoba are as varied as the flora and fauna that visitors can see along the trails. Novice, intermediate and advanced hikers who wish to immerse themselves in the best of Manitoba's natural settings have plenty of options. **Riding Mountain National Park** (page 36) offers hikers relatively easy self-guided trails, such as the Clear Lake Trail, as well as more challenging treks, like the 25-kilometre back-country Birdtail Trail in the northwest corner of the park, near Bob Hill Lake. In **Birds Hill Provincial Park** (page 14), there are theme-specific routes, such as the Cedar Bog Self-Guiding

Trail, White-Tailed Deer Self-Guiding Trail, Chickadee Trail and Bur Oak Self-Guiding Trail. Manitoba also features hikes to unexpected landforms, such as the self-guided Spirit Sands/Devil's Punch Bowl Trail in **Spruce Woods Provincial Park** (page 44) that leads you to sand dunes. At **Oak Hammock Marsh** (page 26), hikers can choose from the marsh's 30-kilometre network of marked trails on relatively easy gravel paths, wooden boardwalks and grass footpaths. Hikers will have a similar experience on the **Grassy Narrows Marsh Trail** (page 18), which winds for about 25 kilometres through protected wetlands that are accessible from Hecla/Grindstone Provincial Park. In the remote northern parts of the province, there are trails that lead to picturesque waterfalls, such as the trail from Pisew Falls to Kwasitchewan Falls in **Pisew Falls Provincial Park** (page 74).

Here are more standout hikes for nature lovers in Manitoba.

## Frank Skinner Arboretum Trail

Hikes for horticulturalists! The Frank Skinner Arboretum Trail passes through what was once an operating arboretum and horticultural centre established in the mid-1920s by Dr. Frank Leith Skinner, one of the most innovative horticulturists and plant propagators of his time. Though the arboretum isn't operating today, the property features one of the most extensive (and oldest) collections of trees and shrubs to have persevered on the Canadian Prairies. There are two self-guided trails that pass through a historic nursery plantation, as well as experimental and native plant gardens where all manner of lilacs, clematis, roses, honeysuckles, trees and shrubs continue to grow. You will find the trail in Dropmore, 1 kilometre west of Provincial Trunk Highway 83, approximately 30 kilometres north of Russell.

## Grey Owl Trail

The 8.9-kilometre Grey Owl Trail (17.8 kilometres return), in the Clear Lake area of Riding Mountain National Park, appeals to history buffs and nature lovers. The trail leads visitors to the original cabin of Parks Canada's first-ever hired naturalist, the enigmatic trapper-turned-conservationist Grey Owl (born Archibald Stansfield Belaney). The trail immerses hikers in forests of aspen, balsam, poplar, jack pine and white spruce. White-tailed deer, coyotes, beavers,

↑ **The challenging Hunt Lake Trail winds through enchanting forests of cedar and eastern white pine.**

muskrats, moose and waterfowl are frequently spotted. The Grey Owl Trail intersects with the Kinosao Trail, which is popular with mountain bikers. Follow Provincial Trunk Highway 10 north from the south gate of Riding Mountain National Park, and then continue east on Provincial Trunk Highway 19 for

↑ **Granite ridges, streams, boreal forests, steep ascents and more await along the 60-kilometre Mantario Trail.**

3 kilometres. The trailhead is on the north side of the road.

**Note:** Don't confuse this trail with the Grey Owl Trail across the border in Saskatchewan's Prince Albert National Park.

## Hunt Lake Trail

A memorable trail in Whiteshell Provincial Park, the 12.6-kilometre (return) back-country Hunt Lake Trail starts at the fishing docks at Hunt Lake and then winds along the east shore of West Hawk Lake north to Little Indian Bay.

Hikers who plan to do this challenging day hike can expect to trek over rocky terrain in the shadow of granite rock faces and through boggy areas of the Canadian Shield, navigating their way through stands of cedars and eastern white pine. The sight of trees growing out of crevices in the rock makes for dramatic photographs. Some parts of the trail, especially where it passes near the cedar bogs, are wet year-round.

## Mantario Hiking Trail

The protected 60-kilometre Mantario Hiking Trail, another trail in Whiteshell Provincial Park, is the longest trail through the Canadian Shield in Western Canada. A section of the trail passes through what's known as the Mantario Wilderness Zone, an area where motorized vehicles, hunting and any kind of development or mining are forbidden.

Expect hilly ascents, bogs, granite ridges, ravines, boreal forests and plenty of lakes. Near Doreen Lake, hikers can see glacial swirl holes in the granite outcrops. Possible wild-life sightings include white-tailed deer, black bears, moose, muskrats, river otters, fishers, minks, beavers, garter snakes, tree frogs, leopard frogs, bald eagles and turkey vultures.

The trail is best suited to experienced backpackers and hikers who are equipped for a multi-day hike. The south trailhead is off Provincial Road 312, east of Caddy Lake, and the north trailhead is located on the north shore of Big Whiteshell Lake, off Provincial Road 309.

## Miami-Thompson Trail

The 55-kilometre Miami-Thompson Trail is actually part of the Great Trail (Trans-Canada Trail). It's a relatively easy trek extending from Thompson to Stanley. The most significant nature highlight is the Manitoba Escarpment, one of the province's few landforms not worn down by glacial activity. Hikers are often joined on the trail by cyclists and horseback riders from the nearby town of Miami. Visitors enjoy excellent views of the lowlands of the Red River Valley from the top of the escarpment — a novelty in a region largely known for its lack of hills.

## Pinawa Trail

Now considered part of the Great Trail as well, this 28-kilometre path in Pinawa Dam Provincial Park offers up an interesting combination of nature highlights (grasslands, beaver dams, granite ridges, mixed forests) alongside such human-made structures as the now-disused hydroelectric dam on the Winnipeg River. The trail includes the Pinawa Channel Heritage Walk, the Ironwood Trail and the Alice Chambers Trail, where hikers will find the 54-metre-long Pinawa Suspension Bridge. Deer and other wildlife are occasionally spotted in the nearby park area. Pinawa Dam is northwest of Pinawa or northeast of Lac du Bonnet on Provincial Road 520.

↑ The 28-kilometre Pinawa Trail in Pinawa Dam Provincial Park takes hikers by the now decommissioned hydroelectric dam on the Winnipeg River.

# Paddling

↑ **The Bloodvein River flows through iconic Canadian Shield, from Woodland Caribou Provincial Park all the way to Lake Winnipeg.**

Paddlers, be they in a kayak or canoe, enjoy a perspective of Manitoba that's different from those captured on foot or from the seat of a vehicle. Picture, if you will, the rock formations nature lovers see from the bow of a canoe in **Whiteshell Provincial Park** (page 48) or the up-close encounters kayakers have with moose while drifting down the Black River in **Nopiming Provincial Park** (page 24).

There are more than 100,000 lakes in Manitoba suited to both beginner and advanced paddlers, as well as gently rolling rivers (for easy paddling) and whitewater routes (for the more experienced). Here are some favourite paddling routes that give access to some of the best-loved nature hot spots in Manitoba.

## Bloodvein River

The remote Bloodvein River, known for waterfalls and rapids, offers unspoiled natural beauty from its source near Red Lake in northwestern Ontario all the way to Lake Winnipeg. Designated a Canadian Heritage River in 1987, Bloodvein winds

through the quintessential Canadian Shield: thick pine forests, exposed granite ridges, moss-covered eskers, boreal forests and a mix of wildlife.

The 200-kilometre Manitoba stretch of the Bloodvein that flows through Atikaki Provincial Park to Lake Winnipeg is "pool and drop," meaning there are calm pools of water between rapids. Paddling experience is essential for this river. Most paddlers fly in by float plane, as there is no decent road access to the Bloodvein. For more information on the river, visit the website for the Canadian Heritage Rivers

System (chrs.ca). Specific details on routes are also available online, at Canadian Canoe Routes (myccr.com).

## Grass River

This subarctic river from Cranberry Portage to Wekusko Falls is popular with seasoned canoeists, many of whom get the opportunity to see the red-ochre pictographs at Tramping Lake. (It's believed they were painted by Indigenous artists while seated in canoes.) One popular stretch is the 565-kilometre route from Cranberry Portage down to

↑ Sasagiu Rapids is a spot along the Grass River that requires portaging — or the skills of a seasoned paddler.

↑ **Paddlers who are looking for a relatively easy day on the water often choose the 11-kilometre Pinawa Channel.**

Split Lake, where the shorelines sometimes reach more than 30 metres high. There's plenty of scenery to admire, such as the dolomite cliffs on the southern shore of Reed Lake. Because of the remoteness, paddling excursions can take experienced canoeists up to two weeks to complete. Some portions of the route are particularly challenging, such as the stretch between Wekusko Lake and Reed Lake, which turns choppy very quickly when a storm hits.

## Manigotagan River

Paddling the Manigotagan River in southeastern Manitoba is an ideal way to explore Manigotagan River Provincial Park. Much of this whitewater river, which flows into the eastern side of Lake Winnipeg, is challenging, though novices — especially when accompanied by seasoned paddlers — have been known to tackle the popular 134-kilometre stretch between Provincial Road 314 and Manigotagan at the mouth of Lake Winnipeg. There are both waterfalls and rapids, while portage routes range from 20 to 450 metres in length. The landscape is made up of sheer granite rock faces, stands of jack pine, balsam poplar and green ash, elderberry bushes, lichen-covered rocks, and the only Canada yew tree found in Manitoba. Wildlife sightings include moose, black bears, wolves, eagles and woodland caribou.

## Pinawa Channel

The Pinawa Channel in southeastern Manitoba, near the town of Pinawa, is one of the most popular daytrip paddling options in the province. The 11-kilometre canoe route, which starts at the Diversion Dam near the town of Pinawa, rewards paddlers with abundant points of interest: cliffs and boulders lining the shore, turtles nesting, plus ducks, geese, eagles and (on occasion) rare trumpeter swans. Expect to see white-tailed deer as well. Paddlers have the option of tackling small rapids or, alternatively, portaging near the suspension bridge. The route ends at the Old Pinawa Dam, the top of which offers excellent views of the surrounding area. As a bonus, no upstream paddling is required.

## Seal River

The Seal River, like the Bloodvein, has been designated a Heritage River. It flows through the heart of northern Manitoba's wilderness, more than 1,000 kilometres north of Winnipeg. This fast-moving river flows from the junction

↑ **The fast-flowing Seal River winds through the heart of northern Manitoba's wilderness.**

of the North and South Seal rivers, at Shethanei Lake, to the Hudson Bay. It's been called one of Manitoba's "last, great un-dammed rivers."

The scenery and wildlife contrast sharply with the nature views paddlers experience in central and southern Manitoba. The route is marked by challenging rapids, boulder-strewn shores and deep gorges, plus sandpits and bars. Up here you're apt to see polar bears, harbour seals and beluga whales as well as wolves, moose and golden and bald eagles. Paddlers typically fly from Winnipeg, Thompson or Gillam to Tadoule Lake, where they begin their 300-kilometre journey downstream to the Hudson Bay.

# Waterfalls

↑ **At 14 metres tall, Kwasitchewan Falls is the highest waterfall in Manitoba.**

For a Prairie province, Manitoba has a surprising number of waterfalls, but it quickly becomes evident that they're concentrated in the northern and easternmost parts of the province.

With a drop of 14 metres, Manitoba's highest waterfall is Kwasitchewan Falls, which surpasses the nearby Pisew Falls by a single metre. These two falls are best visited on an excursion to **Pisew Falls Provincial Park** (page 74), where enthusiasts can also check out the less-dramatic Grassy River Falls. A little farther south, Wekusko Falls in **Wekusko Falls Provincial Park** (page 62) has the distinction of being, at last count, the only waterfall in Manitoba with a pedestrian bridge constructed over it — meaning it's great for photo ops! If you venture close to the Manitoba-Ontario border, there's Tulabi Falls in **Nopiming Provincial Park** (page 24). However, Manitoba's main location for waterfalls is south of Nopiming in Whiteshell Provincial Park. Here, waterfall seekers can get their fill by exploring the following hot spots.

Take extra caution when hiking near waterfalls, especially if the area is rocky or looks slippery. Stick to the designated trails and viewing platforms, and respect fences and signs — they're there for your safety. Winter hikers should be even more vigilant. Ice formations at waterfalls and near water, while photogenic, can be dangerous.

## Acorn Falls and Viburnum Falls

The 8.2-kilometre Pine Point Self-Guiding Trail, located near Pinawa, links Acorn Falls and Viburnum Falls. There's also the Pine Point Rapids, which is viewable from the trail. The Acorn and Viburnum falls do not have the magnitude of the Pisew or Kwasitchewan falls,

↑ **Viburnum Falls, along the Pine Point Self-Guiding Trail, instills moments of quiet reflection in nature.**

but they're a scenic reward after hiking over this rocky section of the Canadian Shield. Don't expect dramatic water currents at either of these "peaceful" falls, but rather enjoy the constant flow of water over granite that's been worn smooth over thousands of years. The trailhead for the Pine Point Self-Guiding Trail can be found off Provincial Road 307.

## McGillivray Falls

Hikers in Whiteshell Provincial Park can follow a self-guided trail to view the rushing rapids between McGillivray Lake and Caddy Lake, known as McGillivray Falls. These cascades are best visited in the spring when the water is flowing with spring run-off. According to geologists, the stream of water that runs out of McGillivray Lake follows a natural channel through the granite that was carved by glaciers 10,000 years ago.

Hikers have the option of taking the shorter 2.8-kilometre loop to the falls or the longer 4.6-kilometre trail, which passes McGillivray Lake. Take caution on the steep rocky inclines, especially when they're wet. The trail-head to the falls is located off Provincial Trunk Highway 44, close to Caddy Lake.

## Rainbow Falls

No hiking is required to check out Rainbow Falls, which is easily accessed by car from the White Lake Resort access road. The falls are popular with swimmers and can also be reached on foot via the 8-kilometre Rainbow Falls Hiking Trail, which starts at Jessica Lake Lodge, cuts through the forest to White Lake Campground and then leads hikers to the scenic falls. Look for White Lake Resort off Provincial Road 307, and follow the signs to White Lake.

## Sturgeon Falls

Sturgeon Falls is a series of rapids that lead into Nutimik Lake. *Nutimik* means "up the river" in Cree. The falls are popular with experienced kayakers and enthusiasts who are eager to try river surfing on stand-up paddleboards. The waves at Sturgeon Falls are formed by a rocky shoal at a narrow point in the river, the gradient of which is a little over 3 metres. Boarders get to paddle their way through waves and a challenging eddy. Sturgeon Falls is located off Provincial Road 307. At the Nutimik Lake Campground, there are signs for Sturgeon Falls boat launch and campsite.

↑ **The gentle Rainbow Falls is popular with swimmers.**

← **The cascading rapids between McGillivray Lake and Caddy Lake are known as McGillivray Falls.**

# Welcome to Saskatchewan

As I sit writing this, I can't help but notice the flurry of bird activity outside my window. It's fall migration time, and even here in Regina it's remarkable the amount of bird life I can see in the span of a few minutes. Warblers, house finches, chickadees, along with a myriad of sparrows and grackles are battling it out in the backyard, competing for seeds before moving on to their winter destinations.

This, of course, is a small sample of just how rich the birdwatching experience is in Saskatchewan. Because it's a major flyway for many breeding species, especially waterfowl, there are so many opportunities to add new birds to your life list.

Clearly I'm a bit bird and wildlife obsessed, so living and travelling in Saskatchewan is perfect — I can get my nature fix no matter where I am in the province.

For years now, I've shared some of the best secrets this province holds (beyond its fabulous wildlife). The Prairie provinces are sadly often overlooked, and while some residents might prefer it that way, my pride for the beauty and incredible natural experiences found here is something I love to share — and the reason I wanted to write this book.

As someone who has lived in Saskatchewan all but one year of her life, I was surprised by how enlightening the exercise of compiling and capturing the province's beautiful natural experiences has been. One thing I learned is that this place is even more diverse than I ever knew — there are so many wild areas to explore that offer adventures people don't often associate with Saskatchewan. I wish I could highlight every remarkable lake, park and experience, but I believe I've done my best to provide a comprehensive overview.

Though a generous amount of space is wide-open plains and rich agricultural lands dotted with hay bales and grain elevators, getting off the Trans-Canada Highway will expose travellers to diverse and beautiful natural landscapes — from badlands, sand dunes and rolling grasslands to boreal forest, numerous lakes (the province boasts over 100,000 of them!), Canadian Shield and more. The array is sure to surprise.

In addition to discovering Saskatchewan's many nature hot spots, you'll learn how such diverse ecosystems have nurtured an abundance of common flora and fauna along with many rarities, such as endemic plants not found anywhere else on the planet, winter-proof scorpions, endangered whooping cranes, at-risk piping plovers and more.

You'll quickly find you need to plan to spend a good amount of time here. From reeling in record-setting monster walleye, paddling historic northern canoe routes once used by fur trade voyageurs and trekking atop sand dunes to digging up bones in the fossil-rich south and retracing the footsteps of Indigenous Peoples who inhabited the province over 10,000 years ago, the recreational possibilities are endless and wide ranging.

My hope through sharing these spots is that you're inspired to explore this nature-rich "Land of Living Skies," which I proudly call my home. Happy travels!

– Jenn Smith Nelson

→ **The northern lights provide a dramatic backdrop for Castle Butte, in southern Saskatchewan.**

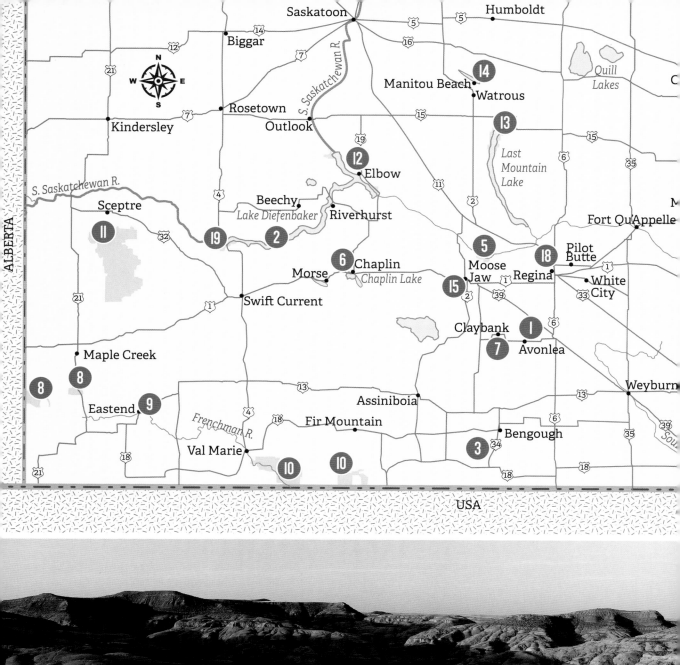

Saskatoon
Humboldt
Biggar
14
12
5
Manitou Beach
Watrous
16
13
Quill Lakes
Rosetown
7
Outlook
15
Kindersley
19
Last Mountain Lake
12
Elbow
S. Saskatchewan R.
Sceptre
11
Beechy
Lake Diefenbaker
Riverhurst
Fort QuAppelle
19
2
5
18
Pilot Butte
6
Chaplin
Moose Jaw
Regina
Morse
Chaplin Lake
15
White City
Swift Current
1
Claybank
1
7
Avonlea
Maple Creek
8
8
Weyburn
13
Eastend
9
Assiniboia
4
18
Fir Mountain
13
6
Val Marie
Frenchman R.
Bengough
3
34
10
10
35
18
18

ALBERTA

USA

# Southern Saskatchewan

# Avonlea Badlands and the Dirt Hills

*Stunning carved pieces of earth stand alongside some of the world's highest glacial push hills*

## What Makes This Hot Spot Hot?

- Hoodoos of textured mudrock and fissured sandstone make up the badlands.
- Part of the Missouri Coteau, the Dirt Hills tower 880 metres above the plains.
- Rocks found at the top of the Dirt Hills date back 75 million years.

**Address:** Avonlea Heritage Museum, 219 Railway Ave, Avonlea, SK
**GPS:** 50.0133; −105.06087
**Tel:** (306) 868-2101
**Website:** avonleamuseum.ca

**Open May to August**

↗ **In the Avonlea Badlands, the passing of time can be seen through linear layers of rock formation.**

The only thing fictional about the Avonlea Badlands is the origin of its name, which comes from the fictitious town in the novel *Anne of Green Gables*. Though these long-standing landscape anomalies may look like something out of a sci-fi movie, Avonlea Badlands and the Dirt Hills are far from make-believe, comprising important features that speak to the geological history of the area.

Tucked away a mere 45 minutes from Regina, these badlands, which lie between Avonlea Creek Valley and the Dirt Hills, are a fragile area of continually eroding textured mudrock and fissured sandstone. Like a gallery of outdoor

monuments, the badlands' hoodoo formations jut from the earth, standing out indifferently against the prairie foundation. A variety of weather-beaten buttes, craggy cliffs and pillar formations fill the landscape.

A few kilometres away and visible from the badlands, the Dirt Hills rise high above the plains at 880 metres. Part of the Missouri Coteau, the hills were formed during the last ice age, some 10,000 to 12,000 years ago, when glaciers dug into the ground and pushed up mounds of dirt known as ice-thrust ridges or glacial push hills. The Dirt Hills, in particular, are some of the largest and most developed push hills in the world, with rocks at the top dating back 75 million years.

Rich in archaeological sites, this hot spot attracts geologists, paleontologists, naturalists and others. But you need not be studious to discover the area — it's an ideal place for hikers to sightsee on foot. Exploring the area is done by guided tour only, as the property is on private land. Visitors can book tours a week in advance through the Avonlea Heritage Museum and choose from a variety of tours depending on specific interests — from archaeology and history to hiking and photography-focused jaunts.

↑ The Dirt Hills were formed during the last ice age and are among the highest push hills in the world.

↓ A hoodoo stands apart from the rocky landscape of the badlands.

# Beechy Sandcastles

*These one-of-a-kind sandstone sandcastles, which have been formed over thousands of years, contrast against the prairie landscape*

## What Makes This Hot Spot Hot?

- Hikers can explore 39 kilometres of the Sunken Hill Trail on foot.
- Prehistoric fossils, such as mussels and oysters, can be found near the water's edge.
- Golden eagles are known to nest in the area, and other common residents include pronghorn antelope, elk, foxes and bull snakes.

**Address:** 7.2 km west of Beechy, SK, on Hwy 342, then 29 km south on Howendale School Rd
**GPS:** 50.65517; –107.5308
**Tel:** (306) 859-2205
**Website:** tourismsaskatchewan.com

**Open year-round, weather permitting (the best time to visit is between June 1 and October 31)**

🚶 🔭 🚴 🦮 🦴

♿ (Limited, check ahead)

↗ **Explorers young and old will enjoy the hiking trails near Sunken Hill.**

It's a safe bet that most people don't associate Saskatchewan and sandcastles. But that is exactly what visitors will find near the small village of Beechy, nestled in the Coteau Hills in the province's southwest.

Located 20 minutes or so from the village, the Beechy Sandcastles are incredible land formations that weave towards the north shore of Lake Diefenbaker. The deeply carved sandstone sculptures are the result of thousands of years of wind and rain erosion on the hills.

A level pasture trail facing the lake is the starting point for hikers. Visitors should be cautious when navigating to and over the sandcastles, as the trail is tricky and has a few steep and unsteady spots. Once carefully through, the view from the rim of the sandcastles showcases a truly

spectacular and rewarding panorama.

Just past the sandcastle trail, a portion of Sunken Hill and the Sunken Hill Trail can be seen and accessed. You can take in the famous disappearing peak that is thought to have been a natural gas pocket that sank suddenly in 1949. Expect dramatic views of the dunes and Lake Diefenbaker along this dirt and gravel trail, which is surrounded by mixed grassland, rolling hills and coulees.

While wandering along cactus- and wildflower-littered pathways to get an up-close-and-personal view of the famed plateau, you can also spot tipi rings. Search along the water's edge for prehistoric fossils, such as mussels and oysters.

This interesting landscape is also home to a whole host of wildlife, including amphibian and bird species. Golden eagles are known to nest along the lake, while pronghorn antelope, elk, foxes, bull snakes, prairie falcons and sharp-tailed grouse are among the common residents that can be spotted.

Though the sandcastles are on private land, you are welcome to explore the area, but you must ensure all gates are closed behind you as this area is a working farm. You should also be aware that, because the trails are dirt and gravel, parts of the trail aren't passable during or after rain. Tourism Saskatchewan advises visitors to call ahead to check on trail conditions before departing.

↑ **Weathered and eroded, the sandcastles are standout features on the shore of Lake Diefenbaker.**

↓ **Prickly pear cacti are found all along the pathways.**

# Big Muddy Badlands and Castle Butte

**This badlands region, equally appealing for both its beauty and ruggedness, was once a refuge for bandits of the Wild West**

## What Makes This Hot Spot Hot?

- With buttes and caves that served as hideouts for outlaws, the Big Muddy Valley is rich in geological and historical significance.
- The area is home to Canada's only known buffalo effigy.
- Many birds of prey live in the area, including golden eagles, prairie falcons and a wide variety of hawks.

**Address:** Hwy 34, 19 km south of Bengough, SK
**GPS:** 49.21756; −105.21906
**Tel:** (306) 267-3312
**Website:** coronach.ca/tours-badlands.html

**Open early May to late September (the best time to visit is July and August)**

&#9855; (Limited, check ahead)

Saskatchewan's Big Muddy Badlands is a popular destination for those hoping to follow in the footsteps of bygone outlaws.

Found 19 kilometres north of the U.S. border, the dramatic landscape of these remote badlands proved ideal for both bank robbers and horse thieves of the late 1800s and early 1900s. Following the Outlaw Trail, which ran from Big Muddy all the way to Mexico, infamous Wild West characters, such as Sam Kelly and Dutch Henry, once used the area's rolling hills, weathered buttes, canyons and caves as hideouts to evade the law.

For how rugged the vast and dry badlands appear, they are just as beautiful. Eroded sandstone caves and ravines, wind-carved buttes and steep cliffs make this area especially photogenic, while also addressing the false notion that Saskatchewan is flat. Big Muddy Valley is an ancient glacial meltwater channel created during the last ice age. As glaciers retreated north, a large quantity of water flowed southeastwards and carved a wide valley with high walls. Over several geological periods, sedimentary layering processes occurred, leaving behind the craggy buttes.

Inside the valley is Castle Butte. This dominant formation on the badlands landscape — made from sandstone, clay, alkali and coal deposits — stands 60 metres high and has a circumference of half a kilometre. Besides its status as a notable geological feature, it was used as a landmark by Plains, Assiniboine and Sioux Lakota nations, along with the North-West Mounted Police, settlers and, most likely, outlaws.

Evidence of early Indigenous settlement is found throughout the area, with tipi rings and ceremonial circles dotting the landscape. Canada's only buffalo effigy,

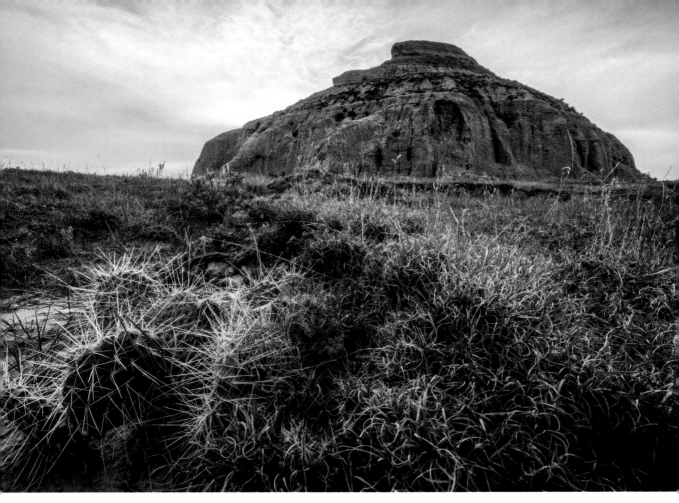

constructed of fieldstones, can also be found. The buffalo effigy is believed to speak to the important relationship between bison and Indigenous Peoples, as well as the spiritual and historical significance of the animal.

If you bring along a pair of binoculars, you may spot birds of prey that are commonly found in the area — from ferruginous, marsh, Cooper's, red-tailed and Swainson's hawks to prairie falcons and golden eagles.

Guided half-day and daylong tours, along with private tours

↑ Though it was used as a hideout, Castle Butte is a massive landmark that's hard to miss.

→ Despite the rocky, desolate-looking terrain, flora flourishes in the Big Muddy area.

(using your own vehicle), of the area showcase the Outlaw Trail, Castle Butte, the caves and more. The badlands are on private land and can only be accessed by booking tours a week in advance through the town of Coronach. Tours run from early May until the end of September.

# Boundary Dam Reservoir

**Legendary largemouth bass draw anglers from both sides of the border to this fast-growing fishing hole**

## What Makes This Hot Spot Hot?

- Boundary Dam Reservoir is the only lake in Saskatchewan that supports a largemouth bass fishery.
- Yellow perch, walleye, trout and northern pike also populate the reservoir.
- Nearby Woodlawn Regional Park offers visitors a variety of outdoor activities and a place to camp.

**Address:** From Estevan, SK, head south on Hwy 47 for approximately 8 km and then 2 km west
**GPS:** 49.07382; –103.02947
**Tel:** (306) 637-3837
**Website:** woodlawnregionalpark.com

**Open year-round; camping is available May long weekend to late September**

&#9826; (Limited, check ahead)

↗ **Boundary Dam is the only place in Saskatchewan to catch largemouth bass.**

Located within the rural municipality of Estevan, Boundary Dam Reservoir attracts fishing fanatics from far and wide. What's all the fuss? It's the go-to lake in the province for landing largemouth bass — actually, it's the only one.

Bass thrive in the reservoir's warm water environment, a result of its proximity to Boundary Dam Power Station, a coal-fired plant south of Estevan. Originally stocked with largemouth bass, this hugely popular lake has become a very healthy fishery.

Midsummer provides the best opportunity to reel in a big bass. There are several access points for Boundary Dam Reservoir, but local anglers swear by the weedier south end and spillway as consistent spots in the warm months. Bass are known to hide in underwater structures, so luring one is easiest by casting into the shallow areas, ideally around dusk or dawn, when the fish are most active.

The average largemouth bass has a lifespan of 16 years. Females are generally larger than males, and they never stop growing. The largest bass caught in the reservoir was recorded in 2016, measuring over 46 centimetres.

The reservoir is also a great spot for ice fishing in the winter. Note, however, that the northern two-thirds of the lake do not freeze over because of the warmth produced by the power station, so be cautious of thin ice.

Other species such as yellow perch, walleye, trout and northern pike can also be caught in the reservoir. Each May, the Estevan Wildlife Federation attracts competitive types for its annual walleye fishing tournament.

Nearby Rafferty Dam on the Souris River is another fishing hole frequented by anglers, especially those who like to fish from shore.

Boundary Dam Beach and close-by Woodlawn Regional Park are fast-growing recreational sites that draw campers and boaters. Split by a flash flood in 2011, Woodlawn Regional Park is now found in both the Boundary Dam and Souris areas. Both sections are great spots to spend the day at the beach swimming, picnicking and boating. Kayak and canoe rentals are available in the Souris portion of the park. Common wildlife spotted in the area includes mule and white-tailed deer, rabbits, porcupines, skunks and the occasional moose.

↑ **The Boundary Dam Power Station, which warms the reservoir, can be seen from the beach.**

↓ **Largemouth bass prefer to hide near underwater structures, like fallen trees.**

# Buffalo Pound Provincial Park

*Nestled in the Qu'Appelle Valley, this glacially formed park is a perfect blend of nature and recreation*

## What Makes This Hot Spot Hot?

- Perfect for birdwatchers, the park offers a huge variety of species, from migrant waterfowl and predatory birds to songbirds.
- A captive herd of plains bison call the park home.
- A mecca for mountain bikers, the area features 32 kilometres of semi-technical trails.

**Address:** Hwy 301, 24 km north of the Trans-Canada Hwy (Hwy 1)
**GPS:** 50.5863; −105.42136
**Tel:** (306) 694-3229
**Website:** tourismsaskatchewan. com/places-to-go

**Open year-round; camping is available May long weekend to late September**

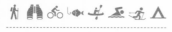

&#9855; (Check ahead)

↗ **A male northern shoveller wades roadside near Buffalo Pound Provincial Park.**

You can see the path of glaciers that moved through the uniform plains over 10,000 years ago, leaving behind uncharacteristic hills centred on a nutrient-rich prairie lake.

Buffalo Pound Provincial Park, the result of such glaciation, has become a tried-and-true four-season recreational destination. The park's rolling hills surround a wetland marsh at the southern tip of the 21-kilometre-long, 500-metre-wide Buffalo Pound Lake.

Nicolle Flats, which is the wetland area, is an interpretive ecological spot. Found near the confluence of the Moose Jaw and Qu'Appelle rivers, it features a marsh boardwalk and several hiking trails. In the summer months, cattails and tall grasses surround the wetlands, which are perfect for canoeing, kayaking and fishing.

The area teems with wildlife and is a prime site for spotting birds, especially migrant waterfowl, predatory birds and songbirds. Residents include coots, grebes, red-tailed hawks, mountain bluebirds, yellow-headed blackbirds, northern shovellers, herons, kingfishers and horned larks. Beavers and muskrats are commonly spotted in dens near the marsh,

and mule and white-tailed deer, foxes and coyotes also bed down in the valley.

Native flora such as prairie sage and common yarrow can be found in patches trailside, with prickly pear cacti dotting the hills.

Reintroduced in 1972, plains bison graze on the area's scenic rolling hills, though as a captive herd. Historically, Indigenous Peoples, such as Atsina, Nakota, Cree and Métis (to name a few), depended on the area's topography to capture bison in corrals or "buffalo pounds," hence the name given to the park in 1963.

Beyond wildlife, recreational activities are a huge draw. Near Nicolle Flats, hikers can choose from several trails,

ranging from 1 to 8 kilometres, that weave through the thick marshland and over valley hills. Several feature rewarding lake views that extend for kilometres. Trails can be accessed from two points near Nicolle Flats — via the east and west trailheads.

Mountain bikers can also take advantage of the old White Track Ski Area. Riders can find their comfort zone with over 30 kilometres of well-marked, semi-technical trails ranging from winding and casual to fast and steep. Trails typically start in the Lower Chalet area where the trailhead map is found. In the winter, many of the biking trails convert into cross-country ski trails.

↑ Autumn is a beautiful time to explore the Qu'Appelle Valley with a hike through Nicolle Flats.

↓ Reintroduced plains bison roam the hills of Buffalo Pound today.

# Chaplin Lake

**With over 100,000 shorebirds arriving each spring, including up to half of the world's sanderlings, this is one of the most important bird migration points in the province**

## What Makes This Hot Spot Hot?

- Chaplin Lake is the second-largest saline lake in Canada.
- Over 30 species of shorebirds visit Chaplin annually, including plovers, avocets, sandpipers and godwits.
- The Chaplin Nature Centre offers a wealth of information on shorebirds as well as guided tours.

**Address:** Off the Trans-Canada Hwy (Hwy 1) near Chaplin, SK
**GPS:** 50.4566; –106.65952
**Tel:** (306) 395-2770
**Website:** chaplintourism.com

**Open early May to early September**

&#9855; (Limited, check ahead)

↗ A large variety of shorebirds gather and intermingle in the saline waters.

Bordering the rural village of Chaplin, along the Trans-Canada Highway, at 20 square kilometres Chaplin Lake is the second-largest saline water body in Canada and an important migratory point that's jam-packed with birds.

Besides being a source of high-quality sodium sulphate (the white stuff you see along the road), the lake is a significant shorebird-nesting habitat. In 1997, it was designated a site of hemispheric importance, the highest designation possible by the Western Hemisphere Shorebird Reserve Network (WHSRN). To merit this designation, a site must host at least 500,000 shorebirds annually or 30 per cent of the population of a single species, and Chaplin is one of only three such sites in Canada.

Each year thousands of visitors and hundreds of birders flock to Chaplin Lake, hoping to add to their life lists from the over 30 species of shorebirds that visit the sandy marshlands. Which bird tops the list? Most often, it's the endangered piping plover. One-third of this at-risk species are found in Canada, with

Saskatchewan noted as a major nesting area for the small birds.

Other notable seasonal visitors include at times up to half the world's population of sanderlings, the stunningly marked American avocets, stilt sandpipers, marbled godwits and killdeer.

Mid-May is the optimal time for visiting. Birds that pit stop in Chaplin then come by the thousands, with some returning in August and September followed by their young. Many, such as the plovers, come to nest. Others, like sanderlings and semipalmated sandpipers, come to fuel up en route to their Arctic breeding grounds. This pattern has repeated for thousands of years, and with so few predators in the area to be concerned about, they can fatten up in peace in preparation for the next long haul. In a fluster of intermingled avian activity, shorebirds feast on brine shrimp, brine flies and insects found along the salty shores and shallow waters.

Though shorebirds are the star attractions, other exceptional and threatened bird species can be spotted amid the surrounding prairie land, including burrowing owls, ferruginous hawks and long-billed curlews.

You can do a self-guided tour, but it's limited to one stretch of road along Highway 58. Due to private roads with restricted access, your best bet is to take a guided tour of the lake's best vantage points, which provide up-close viewing of the birds and their nesting areas. Tours can be booked through the Chaplin Nature Centre.

If you continue 20 minutes west along the Trans-Canada Highway to Reed Lake, also part of the WHSRN-designated area, you'll find a viewing tower just west of Morse that allows you to scan the bird-filled landscape from above.

↑ The wind kicks up clouds of salt along a sodium sulphate-lined private road, which can only be accessed through guided tours.

↓↓ American avocets are easy to spot at Chaplin Lake.

↓ The piping plover, a species at risk, nests on Chaplin Lake.

# Claybank Brick Plant National Historic Site

**Frozen in time, this clay-rich area provides lessons about the area's once-flourishing brick industry and is also a retreat for hikers and wildlife enthusiasts**

## What Makes This Hot Spot Hot?

- The area was a historical source of whitemud clay that was formed during the Cretaceous period.
- Hikers can explore the Massold Clay Canyons, a 103-hectare wildlife area where clay was once extracted.
- Common flora found in the area includes prairie crocuses, willows, roses and a variety of wild berries.

**Address:** Hwy 339, 1 km east of Claybank, SK
**GPS:** 50.0321; −105.21413
**Tel:** (306) 868-4474
**Website:** claybankbrick.ca

**Open June to August**

   🚹 👓

♿ (Limited, check ahead)

↗ **Impeccably preserved, Claybank Brick Plant immerses you in the brick-making process.**

Amid rolling hills and grassy plains, at the foot of the Dirt Hills, sits the Claybank Brick Plant National Historic Site, an area that once thrived economically thanks to its abundance of unique fireclay.

Designated a National Historic Site back in 1994, Claybank has aged gracefully — withstanding the test of time, much like its products — and remains one of the best-preserved brick plants of its era in North America.

You can expect an immersive exploration of the plant's history as the site has been frozen in time from the 1920s. All of the crucial components used in every stage of brick manufacturing, along with 95 per cent of its original structures (think giant kilns), have been retained and are showcased. You will discover how, over the course of nearly eight decades, the plant created and supplied heat-resistant firebricks worldwide until its

↑ It's easy to spot the pits where high-refractory clay was once extracted.

closing in 1989. The plant's fire-bricks were used everywhere from the historic Chateau Frontenac in Quebec City to World War II warships to the rocket launch pads at Cape Canaveral.

Though they are hidden in the distance, the Massold Clay Canyons, which are the clay extraction pits, can be viewed. This adjacent area once supplied two types of high-refractory clay — meaning clay that can withstand high levels of heat, which is perfect for brick and tile. The clay was formed during the Cretaceous period (which began 145 million years ago and ended 66 million years ago) and is aptly known as whitemud. It can be seen in the white stripes rippling across the canyon walls.

Besides being a historical source of clay, the canyons serve as a 103-hectare wildlife area that begs exploration. Hikers often make a day of it trekking through the canyons. The area has never been cultivated, so as a result it is home to several species of native flora, including prairie crocuses, willows, roses, buffalo berries, wild strawberries and gooseberries. Because of its vegetation and elevation, a great variety of wildlife and birds, such as ruby-throated hummingbirds, downy woodpeckers and mountain bluebirds, are attracted to this habitat.

Hiking is included in the price of touring Claybank, but a day pass or annual membership can also be purchased.

# Cypress Hills Interprovincial Park

*Canada's first interprovincial park features the highest points of land between the Rockies and Labrador's Torngat Mountains*

## What Makes This Hot Spot Hot?

- More than 730 plant species grow in Cypress Hills.
- The park is a designated Dark-Sky Preserve.
- The Conglomerate Cliffs and Hidden Conglomerate Cliffs are must-see natural attractions within the park's West Block.

**Addresses:** Centre Block: Ben Nevis Dr, Maple Creek, SK
West Block: Hwy 271, approximately 55 km south of Maple Creek, SK
**GPS:**
Centre Block: 49.66037; –109.50174
West Block: 49.57552; –109.87378
**Tel:** (306) 662-5411
**Website:** cypresshills.com

**Centre Block is open year-round; West Block is open May long weekend to Labour Day**

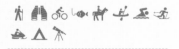

 (Check ahead)

Straddling Saskatchewan and Alberta, Cypress Hills was designated Canada's first interprovincial park in 1989. But that's not all it's known for. Anyone who thinks Saskatchewan is flat will be quickly proven wrong when they learn that the tallest peak in the Saskatchewan portion of the park, standing at 1,392 metres above sea level, makes it one of the highest points in Canada east of the Canadian Rockies.

Virtually untouched by glaciers during the last ice age, Cypress Hills is brimming with rugged beauty, seen in the park's deep valleys and vast forests. It also features flora, fauna and vistas akin to the Rockies.

Don't, however, let the name fool you. The park isn't home to any cypress trees. Instead, its forests are densely packed with incredibly straight — not to mention tall (up to 18 metres!) — lodgepole pines that pop up from the surrounding prairie panorama. A mistake made by early French fur traders who misidentified the trees resulted in the park's name.

Long known as a gathering place, for centuries people have camped out on Cypress Hills' knolls, relying on its resources, especially its trees. Trunks of the tall pines made excellent travois, and First Nations, such as Cree, Dakota and Blackfoot Confederacy nations, used the lodgepole pines for tipi poles and lodges.

In addition to the pines, the park's flora is quite remarkable, with over 730 plant species and 20 per cent of those species considered rare and unique. This number includes uncommon orchids such as the bog, the lady's tresses and the Venus's slipper, to name a few.

Over 40 species of mammals call the park home, and sightings of moose and white-tailed deer are common both roadside and within the campsites. Other residents include coyotes, bobcats, pronghorn antelopes and the highest density

of cougars found in North America. These predators were extirpated from the area for over 100 years, only to return on their own in the 1990s. Cypress Hills is also a birder's paradise, with 220 species recorded in the park. Birders will relish seeing everything from golden eagles, sharp-tailed grouse and wild turkeys to trumpeter swans and songbirds.

The park is divided into two blocks — Centre Block and West Block — and each is full of diverse appeal.

## Centre Block

Centre Block, approximately 20 minutes from the town of Maple Creek, is the most developed side of the park and offers the majority of visitor services. It's also where most people tend to set up camp, as sites are close to park amenities. With five campgrounds and 600-plus campsites to choose from, you can have your choice of basic to full service camping. Group campgrounds are available as well.

Families flock to Loch Leven, also known as the beach, where days are spent enjoying popular activities such as swimming, paddle boating and canoeing.

For trail enthusiasts, Centre Block has a trail network that spans 27 kilometres, with most trailheads found in the core area. There are several hiking and biking trails that average 1 to 2 kilometres. Hike the 2-kilometre Native Prairie Trail, which features both grasslands and mixed-grass and fescue prairie. Experienced hikers will find their challenge along the rugged 16-kilometre part of the Great Trail (Trans-Canada Trail) that stretches between both blocks of Cypress Hills.

↑ **A white-tailed deer weaves through a forest of lodgepole pines.**

↓ **Centre Block has a trail network of 27 kilometres, which is perfect for biking.**

↑ **The view from Bald Butte, the highest point in Centre Block, doesn't disappoint.**

Trail access continues in the winter for cross-country skiing enthusiasts. Centre Block features 16 kilometres of regularly groomed trails that range from novice to intermediate, and cross-country ski rentals are available. Centre Block also has an outdoor hockey rink and designated snowmobiling area. (Snowmobiling is not permitted in West Block.)

Other activities in Centre Block include geocaching and stargazing at the Dark Sky Observatory (a short drive away). Cypress Hills is a designated Dark-Sky Preserve, and the park's observatory offers some of the best stargazing in the province thanks to its light-pollution-free night sky. For remarkable day views, drive to Lookout Point or nearby Bald Butte, the highest point in Centre Block at 1,281 metres.

## West Block

Considered more of a wilderness area and about an hour's drive from Centre Block, West Block offers seasonal rustic camping along Battle Creek and is one of three provincial parks in Saskatchewan to offer equestrian camping, complete with corrals, stalls and more. With nearly 135 square kilometres of forest, grasslands and rolling hills, this unspoiled area offers plenty of diversity to those who want to explore via horseback.

Though the aforementioned portion of the Great Trail between Centre Block and West Block is considered difficult, following it rewards hikers with incredible views. One such highlight, accessible only from the trail, is the view from the Hidden Conglomerate Cliffs, which offer a sweeping panorama of the area. The cliffs are made up of gravel and smooth stones called "cobbles." West Block is home to another set of sedimentary formations called the Conglomerate Cliffs, which can be accessed by vehicle and offer equally stunning views above Adam's Lake. Please note that if there is a fire ban in effect, access is limited to hiking only.

If you are up for a little adventure, find your way to the Mystery Rocks. Found on private land to the south of West Block, this unique rock formation's origin is not known. Some believe this is a magical spot, and many say the rocks induce odd or eerie feelings. Call the landowner first at (306) 299-4514 for permission to access the land and directions to the rocks.

More interested in fact-based history? Take a step back in time to the 1870s at Fort Walsh National Historic Site. If you visit between May 29 and September 29, you can learn the history of the area through tours, demonstrations and interactive workshops. Geocaching, cycling and hiking can all be enjoyed at Fort Walsh.

↗ **Dense forest, deep valleys and stunning vistas can be found in Cypress Hills.**

→ **The Conglomerate Cliffs are a breathtaking attraction in West Block.**

# Eastend and the T.rex Discovery Centre

**Fossils, rich wildlife and unique land formations make the "hidden secrets" in this valley worth discovering**

## What Makes This Hot Spot Hot?

- Rich in dinosaur fossils, the area is well known as the home of "Scotty," a 65-million-year-old female *Tyrannosaurus rex.*
- Visitors can drive to points of interest like Chocolate Peak, Chimney Coulee and Jones Peak along one of Eastend's Auto Tours.
- Commonly spotted ungulates include pronghorn antelope and mule and white-tailed deer.

**Address:** Eastend, SK
**GPS:** 49.52223; –108.82824
**Tel:** (306) 295-3322
**Websites:** townofeastend.com, royalsaskmuseum.ca/trex

**Open year-round; the T.rex Discovery Centre is open May long weekend to Labour Day**

&#9855; (Limited, check ahead)

Dropped down into the glacier-carved valley of the Frenchman River, the picturesque area of Eastend is commonly referred to as the Valley of Hidden Secrets thanks to the area's rich amount of fossils and lesser-known points of interest.

Once upon a time, Eastend was a lush tropical environment — one that attracted a variety of life forms, including dinosaurs. Today, it is best known for the 1994 discovery of a female *Tyrannosaurus rex* skeleton. Nicknamed "Scotty," the 65-million-year-old remains make up the most complete fossilized skeleton found in Canada and the ninth largest in the world. Rumour has it that Scotty earned her name from the bottle of Scotch that was consumed while celebrating her find. As the official fossil of Saskatchewan, Scotty can be viewed at the T.rex Discovery Centre, a satellite branch of the Royal Saskatchewan Museum.

Nearly impossible to miss, the semi-circular building juts out conspicuously from the side of a hill overlooking the town of Eastend. You can watch a film on dinosaur hunting or take part in a hands-on fossil excavation or a fossil workshop with a paleontologist. Facility tours are offered every hour.

Other attractions in town include the Eastend Historical Museum, which features artifacts found by the first fossil hunter in the area, Corky Jones. One of the earliest European settlers in the region, Jones founded the museum with his collection of locally discovered fossils, including dinosaur bones.

There's more to Eastend than old bones, however. With vegetation mimicking that of foothills rather than the surrounding prairie, the beautiful yet rugged area teems with wildlife, especially ungulates, such as pronghorn antelope and mule and white-tailed

deer. Streams in the area are perfect for fly-fishing, and the reservoir provides an excellent habitat for ducks and geese.

Unique land formations surround the area, so after you've filled up on dino history, it's time to take to the open road on one or more of Eastend's Auto Tours. (See the Town of Eastend website for more information and maps.)

Drive by obscure and interesting sites, such as Chocolate Peak. The now reddish-brown hill was once referred to as Wedding Cake Hill because of its whitemud clay base. The whitemud deposit was ruined thanks to a miner who attempted to burn the layer of coal found above the deposit in order to get at the mud. Along the same tour, you'll also spot the White Mud Pits, a former mining site that is made up of layers and layers of whitemud, gravel, pebbles and sand. Due to the abundance of whitemud in the area, the region is home to a number of potters who continue to source clay directly from the surrounding cliffs. Another highlight found on this driving route is Jones Peak (named after Corky Jones), where after a short hike you can take in one of Saskatchewan's most magnificent views overlooking the valley and countryside.

Along a different Auto Tour route, you can get out and explore the historical Chimney

Coulee. Named for stone chimneys that are the last remnants of a Métis settlement, the site was formerly a Hudson's Bay Company trading post that was established in 1871.

↑ Getting up above the prairies offers incredible views of the open landscape.

↑↑ Scotty, the ninth-largest *Tyrannosaurus rex* fossil ever found, was discovered in Eastend.

# Grasslands National Park

*Sleep in a tipi, howl with coyotes and experience true conservation in action in the only national park featuring prairie grasslands*

## What Makes This Hot Spot Hot?

- Several rare and endangered native species have been reintroduced into the area.
- Hikers can explore a valley once dominated by dinosaurs.
- The Ecotour Scenic Drive takes visitors past interesting landforms, animal colonies and more.

**Address:** East Block Visitor Centre (McGowan Visitor Centre): Waverley No. 44, Fir Mountain, SK
West Block Visitor Centre: 101 Centre St, Val Marie, SK
**GPS:**
East Block: 49.07136; −106.52961
West Block: 49.245769; −107.732181
**Tel:** East Block: (306) 476-2018
West Block: (1-877) 345-2257
**Website:** pc.gc.ca/en/pn-np

**Open year-round**

♿ (Limited, check ahead)

There may be no better place in Saskatchewan to enjoy the province's iconic wide-open prairie space than Grasslands National Park. It's arguably the province's best spot to witness the "Land of Living Skies" by night, as it is one of Canada's darkest Dark-Sky Preserves. It's also the only national park to represent the prairie grasslands natural region.

Created by erosion from glacial meltwater, the park area features a mix of open grasslands, stunning buttes, rolling hills, coulees and scenic vistas of the Frenchman River Valley. Its plains are also littered with unique land formations and jam-packed with rare flora as well as a mix of water, land and sky critters.

The plains bison, the swift fox and the black-footed ferret are among the endangered native species that have been reintroduced into the area. Grasslands National

Park is also home to 20 at-risk species. Resident mammals, such as badgers, coyotes, and pronghorn antelopes, as well as reptiles, including prairie rattlesnakes, can be spotted throughout the park. Dusk and dawn are the best times of day to look for fauna, as there isn't a lot of respite from the sun, especially during scorching summer days.

The park is a birdwatching hot spot year-round. Look for spotted towhees in riparian shrubs, rock wrens in the badlands, and golden eagles in the buttes. Year-round residents like the endangered greater sage grouse and sharp-tailed grouse are best viewed in spring, while summer provides the perfect chance to see the vulnerable long-billed curlews, longspurs and Sprague's pipits.

Stop at the visitor centres to learn about the variety of events, self-guided tours and interpretive and junior naturalist programs in the park. Many activities are available, from geocaching, mountain biking (note: there are no designated trails) and horseback riding to paddling.

Between the park's two blocks, you'll find diverse activities that make each area an excellent choice to explore in its own right. As the current park holdings are over 700 square kilometres, plan ahead, and take your time touring these incredible grasslands over several days or trips.

## East Block

Get your hands dirty digging for fossils in the badlands of East Block. Much like nearby Eastend (page 118), the eroding

↑ The eroded buttes and exposed badland formations found in East Block are ruggedly beautiful.

← Plains bison were reintroduced to the park in December 2005.

↓ The endangered greater short-horned lizard is a master at camouflage.

layers of earth are dense with 65-million-year-old (and older) fossils of dinosaurs and ancient sea dwellers. Guided digs take place during annual summer events centred on fossil discovery.

Hikers can choose from six front-country hiking trails with easy loops ranging from 1.3 to 2.5 kilometres. They include the Creek to Peak Trail, Rock Creek Trail and Rim Walk Trail. The moderately rated 11-kilometre Zahursky Ridge Trail loop rewards hikers with a view of the badlands.

Another outstanding trek that's popular with experienced hikers is the East Block's Valley of 1,000 Devils. Take in the landscape of striped red-clay hoodoos while roaming the 800-hectare valley of badlands where dinosaurs once dominated. This trail is rated difficult and is 12 kilometres out and back. Keep an eye out for patches of quicksand (yes, really!) and the greater short-horned lizard. If you are very lucky, these endangered reptiles can be spotted in the Frenchman Valley.

East Block is home to the McGowan Visitor Centre (open May long weekend to Thanksgiving long weekend), and within Rock Creek Campground, there are a good number of front-country camping options. In addition to 24 tent and RV sites, cool Parks Canada accommodations include eight oTENTiks (a cross between a tent and a cabin) and three tipis. There are no designated backcountry sites, though backcountry camping is permitted. Visit the Parks Canada website for information on what to expect, and register in person at the visitor centre prior to setting out on your backcountry adventure.

## West Block

If you've happened upon a bison roadblock, you've entered the West Block. In addition to incredible landscapes and archaeologically significant sites, West Block is chock full of wildlife. The best way to take it all in is with the Ecotour Scenic Drive — a 2.5 hour, 80-kilometre self-guided drive along Ecotour Road. Historical homesteads, important archaeological sites, interesting land formations, animal colonies and a rubbing stone are all stops to explore during the driving tour.

One of the cutest (and noisiest) stops is at a black-tailed prairie dog colony. Grasslands National Park and the adjacent lands are the only places they live in Canada. Here, quirky antics and the sophisticated chirps of these native prairie dwellers reign supreme. Endangered burrowing owls can often be spotted on or near the colonies, as they take over abandoned burrows.

↑ Black-tailed prairie dogs are a keystone species as their population health has impacts on numerous other species.

↑↑ The tipi accommodations in West Block offer panoramic views of the open prairie and rolling hills.

West Block boasts 12 front-country hiking trails that offer a variety of views and focal points. Over 12,000 ancient tipi rings are scattered throughout the park, and you can hike the easy 2-kilometre Tipi Ridge Trail loop to view a few of them. For those who want to get to know the park's flora, Eagle Butte Trail showcases both common and rare species along a moderate 2.1-kilometre loop. A historical favourite of bison, blue grama grass is quite easy to find on this trail, as are needle-and-thread grass and prickly pear cacti. Plant lovers should also look for gumbo evening primrose, with flowers that change colour in the evenings. For those who are up for a challenge, the hike to 70 Mile Butte will not disappoint. This 4.1-kilometre loop guides hikers to one of the highest points in the park and offers spectacular views.

Like East Block, there are a variety of accommodations in the scenic Frenchman River Campground, which delivers views of the river, rolling hills and, sometimes, even bison. There are 20 electrical front-country camping sites and four oTENTiks. Tipi rentals are also available at the Two Trees Day-Use Area. Several designated sites for backcountry camping also exist in West Block. All reservations can be made online or at the visitor centre, which is open early May to Thanksgiving long weekend.

Equestrian camping with access to water, horse pens and more is also available in both blocks. In West Block, equestrian sites can be found south of the Belza Day-Use Area, and in East Block, sites are found in Rock Creek Campground.

↑ The hike to 70 Mile Butte is one of the best spots in the park to take in the sunset.

↓ The flowers of grama grass look like long grey eyelashes.

# The Great Sandhills

*One of Canada's largest sets of active sand dunes, this somewhat hidden land formation is definitely worth seeking out*

## What Makes This Hot Spot Hot?

- The dunes measure over 15 metres high in places.
- Over 150 bird species and 20 types of mammals can be spotted.
- The dunes are the perfect environment for the endangered Ord's kangaroo rat, which nests in the area.

**Address:** Turn south on the first grid road west of Sceptre off Hwy 32, then drive approximately 22 km south to the Great Sandhills; watch for signs and a parking lot
**GPS:** 50.69368; −109.28238
**Tel:** (306) 623-4345
**Website:** greatsandhillsmuseum.com

**Open year-round, weather permitting**

↗ **Boot Hill greets you from the parking lot.**

For those who have never been to Saskatchewan, imagining that a desert-like habitat exists in the middle of the Prairies might be hard to fathom. However, the Great Sandhills, in the province's southwest, is one of multiple sets of active sand dunes in Saskatchewan and one of Canada's largest. Protected within the Great Sandhills Ecological Reserve, sand-covered hills tower above an impressive 1,900 square kilometres of terrain. Thanks to wind, this desert-type terrain is perpetually shifting and changing.

Accessing the dunes can be tricky (you might need to ask for directions at the Great Sandhills Museum in Sceptre), but once you've found the parking lot with trail signage directing you up the dunes, you've arrived. Before spotting the sand, you'll be greeted by "Boot Hill," a unique and charming gateway covered in boots made by local rancher John Both (now passed). Ranching is an activity that has long occurred in the area, so don't be surprised if you see or hear cattle.

The trail to the dunes is spotted from Boot Hill, and a 500-metre walk will get you to the top of the closest dune.

The thing to do once on the dunes is to kick off your shoes and feel the surprisingly soft sand between your toes. Don't underestimate the difficulty of hiking along the trails and

on top of the soft sand dunes. If you are up for the challenge, head for the longer dunes found just east of Boot Hill.

While navigating the mounds, look for native grasses, such as sagebrush, along with stunted shrubs that are clinging to life. Some aspen, birch and even willow trees surround the area.

Many mammals are around that are commonly found in the southwest, like coyotes, foxes, weasels, porcupines, pronghorn antelopes and both mule and white-tailed deer. There's also some rare wildlife hidden in the dunes. The endangered Ord's kangaroo rat nests in the area, requiring sparsely vegetated and actively eroding sand dunes for its habitat. While in the area,

bird enthusiasts can look for the fittingly named sandhill crane, as well as short-eared owls and peregrine falcons.

The massive reserve offers simple but beautiful vistas that stretch for kilometres. Saskatchewan's big sky as the backdrop against the expanse of sand makes for fabulous photo compositions, so it's worth bringing your camera along for the trek.

Bear in mind it's easy to get turned around in the Great Sandhills, so bring a compass along. This area doesn't have bathrooms, and camping and fires aren't permitted. You should also avoid the area if it's raining, as the dirt roads leading to the site can be difficult to pass.

↑ The desert-like terrain makes you feel like you are far from Saskatchewan.

↓ Hard to spot because they are tiny (and nocturnal), the rare Ord's kangaroo rat nests in the sand dunes.

# Lake Diefenbaker East

**The eastern portion of the immense Lake Diefenbaker is home to the Gardiner Dam, two provincial parks and endless outdoor opportunities**

## What Makes This Hot Spot Hot?

- With 800 kilometres of shoreline and an array of water-based activities, Lake Diefenbaker is the star attraction of the area.
- Danielson Provincial Park boasts large campsites and great hikes.
- Douglas Provincial Park features massive sand dunes along its popular Cacti Trail.

**Address:** Near Elbow, SK
**GPS:** Danielson Provincial Park: 51.2596; –106.80275
Douglas Provincial Park: 51.0364; –106.4831
**Tel:** Danielson Provincial Park: (306) 857-5510
Douglas Provincial Park: (306) 854-6266
**Website:** tourismsaskatchewan.com/places-to-go

**Open year-round; full services for both parks are available May long weekend to Labour Day**

&#9855; (Limited, check ahead)

Southwest Saskatchewan's largest body of water is often touted as the province's "Great Lake." Lake Diefenbaker was created in 1968, the crown jewel formed thanks to the damming of the Qu'Appelle and South Saskatch-ewan rivers. Today visitors can drive across the iconic Gardiner Dam, recognized as the largest earth-filled dam in Canada (and one of the world's largest). The dam is the province's biggest piece of infrastructure, playing a vital role in water supply and renewable energy.

Transforming two rivers into one massive 220-kilometre long, 66-metre deep lake forever changed the landscape into an area where recreation and nature go hand in hand.

Lake Diefenbaker is undoubtedly what draws scores of visitors and campers to the area, most prolifically for water-based activities, such as sailing, canoeing, windsurfing and wakeboarding. Renting the Betty Lou tour boat is another fun way to spend the day on the water. Take a fully escorted sightseeing tour with up to 40 guests.

Known for its world-class fishing, Lake Diefenbaker is also a favourite jaunt among anglers. It offers a great variety of scaly life forms, from monster trout and trophy walleye to northern pike and world-record rainbow trout. Head to the tailwater of the dam where larger fish feed on baitfish that have been stunned by the heavy water. Several fishing tournaments take place throughout both the summer and winter.

Danielson, Douglas and Saskatchewan Landing pro-vincial parks share the nearly 800-kilometre shoreline, along with a handful of regional parks and agricultural land. Danielson and Douglas border the eastern portion of Lake Diefenbaker, and they're close enough to explore together.

## Danielson Provincial Park

Danielson Provincial Park, sit-uated adjacent to the Gardiner Dam, is a well-loved summer destination for recreation.

Generously sized campsites and a plenitude of activities both on land and water are

the main reasons scores of visitors arrive every summer, particularly families who love to spend time on its unspoiled sandy beach.

Hiking and biking through coulees, woodland and wetland are great ways to pass the time back on land. A 13-kilometre section of the Great Trail (Trans-Canada Trail), which runs the whole length of the park from the southeastern tip to the Gardiner Dam, boasts beautiful lake views, and the Prairie View Trail is connected to the campground. The paths are widely used, so expect easy to moderate hikes that deliver brilliant lake views and wildlife-watching opportunities.

You might see large colonies of pelicans on the lake, which make for a dazzling display of white out on the water. Common amphibious mammals, like beavers, muskrats and minks, are frequently

↑ With Diefenbaker's long sandy coastlines, families often make a day of it at the beach.

↖ Sailing is a popular pastime on Lake Diefenbaker.

↑ Danielson Provincial Park is home to thirteen-lined ground squirrels, which are most active during warm sunny days.

↑↑ Chokecherries and Saskatoon berries can be found in Douglas Provincial Park.

↗ Running the whole length of Danielson Provincial Park, a 13-kilometre section of the Great Trail is popular with hikers.

spotted on the trails. Badgers, raccoons and rodents, such as Richardson's ground squirrels, thirteen-lined ground squirrels and northern pocket gophers, are all found in the park, alongside abundant populations of both mule and white-tailed deer.

Plenty of native flora can also be found in the park, including trembling aspen, creeping juniper, wolf willow, snowberry, bearberry and sand reed grass.

## Douglas Provincial Park

Named after Saskatchewan Premier Tommy Douglas, the late father of Canada's health care system, Douglas Provincial Park is found on Lake Diefenbaker's southeast end. Like its lakeside counterparts, Danielson and Saskatchewan Landing provincial parks, it features a long sandy shoreline and plenty of outdoor adventures. Visitors to the park also enjoy the privacy of heavily wooded campsites and the idyllic beach bursting with water-based activities. However, the park stands apart thanks to a set of massive inland sand dunes and the wonderful interpretive hiking trails that explore them.

One of the most widely used trails in Douglas, the Cacti Trail, found in the northeast area of the park, is 6 kilometres long and rated moderate for difficulty. Hike this trail for access to the 1-kilometre-long (and 30-metre-high) active dune site. Climb the exposed dunes, remnants of a massive lake that once covered the area, for a 360-degree panorama of the sandy landscape. It's not all sand, though. There are also a surprising abundance of birds, such as least flycatchers, clay-coloured sparrows and yellow-bellied sapsuckers, along with stunted vegetation on the dunes.

The park encompasses diverse ecosystems, including moist meadow areas where black poplar and river birch thrive along with unique plants, such as the yellow lady's slipper. Prairie areas feature bluffs of aspen, chokecherries and Saskatoon berries.

Another trail worth hiking is the Great Trail. Passing through the park along the lake from the resort village of Mistusinne, it leads hikers north towards Danielson

Provincial Park. Amble along open prairie, aspen groves and then for kilometres along Diefenbaker's shore. Eagles are often sighted, and deer and coyote tracks dot the beach, so remember to look up and down.

↑ **Hike the Cacti Trail to access active sand dunes in Douglas Provincial Park.**

# Last Mountain Lake National Wildlife Area

*Serving as a much-loved lake to several resort communities, Last Mountain Lake is home to some of the province's best birdwatching and fishing spots*

## What Makes This Hot Spot Hot?

- The area is home to North America's oldest bird sanctuary.
- The observatory at Last Mountain Regional Park is the only migrant bird-banding station in Saskatchewan open to the public.
- The area is home to nine out of Canada's 36 vulnerable bird species, including the piping plover.

**Address:** At Hwy 2 and Hwy 15, drive east on Hwy 15 for 14.4 km until you see a sign for the National Wildlife Area, and then turn south and travel 3.2 km
**GPS:** 51.416929; –105.239036
**Tel:** (306) 484-4483
**Website:** saskregionalparks. ca/park/last-mountain

**The lake is open year-round; Last Mountain Regional Park is open May to September**

&#9855; (Limited, check ahead)

If there's one area in south-western Saskatchewan that's gone to the birds (and the fish), it's Last Mountain Lake, also known as Long Lake. Created by glaciation some 11,000 years ago, this productive lake is the largest naturally occurring body of water in southern Saskatchewan.

It's also home to many popular year-round resort communities, such as Regina Beach, Saskatchewan Beach, Grandview Beach and Rowan's Ravine. Just 30 minutes from Regina, these lakeside getaways attract cabin and beach folks, who flock there to dip their toes in water, head out on a boat for some wakeboarding or reel in a big one on a weekday evening.

But let's get back to the birds. The north end of Last Mountain Lake (near Last Mountain Regional Park) is home to North America's oldest bird sanctuary. Back in 1887, approximately 1,012 hectares adjacent to the shoreline were reserved as a breeding ground for wildfowl, and by 1921 the area officially became the Last Mountain Lake Migratory Bird Sanctuary. It's also a National Historic Site of Canada, designated in 1987.

Mud flats, marshes and northern mixed grasslands make up the protected Last Mountain Lake National Wildlife Area, and for migratory birds, it's the place to be — and to breed. The park is also home to nine out of Canada's 36 vulnerable bird species, including the peregrine falcon and piping plover.

The shallow, wetland-abundant area is where most of the waterfowl nesting occurs, attracting 60 species of nesting birds. Significant numbers of ducks, geese (snow, Ross's and Canada) and sandhill cranes can be found. Endangered whooping cranes have also been spotted during spring and fall migrations.

The fall migration is a sight to behold (and hear) when the honks and trills of over 200,000 ducks and upwards of 400,000 snow geese fill the air. Some years, pelican colonies exceed over 1,000 nests. Other colonial visitors include common and Forster's terns, double-crested cormorants and ring-billed and California gulls.

Many bird and wildlife species can be spotted year-round, including grey partridges and sharp-tailed grouse, as well as white-tailed deer, red foxes, coyotes, white-tailed jackrabbits and badgers.

A great way to take in the birds is to hike the 2-hour self-guided Last Mountain Regional Park Nature Trail. Start at the nature centre near the Last Mountain Bird Observatory, where you'll find a bison rubbing rock and a bird blind to hide behind. While on the trail, look for even more species, such as orchard orioles, kingbirds and yellow-rumped warblers.

For those wanting an even closer look at the birds, the park's observatory features the only migrant bird-banding station in Saskatchewan that's open to the public. Banding takes place during the migration months of May, August and September.

The lake is also a rich fish-spawning area and nursery ground. Several species flourish in the abundant streams and shallow waters, such as the vulnerable bigmouth buffalo, a member of the sucker family. As popular as birdwatching is in the lake's north end, so too is fishing. This is the spawning area of the commonly eaten walleye. There's also a lot of angling action around the south end of the lake. For perch and pike (and more walleye), head to Rowan's Ravine.

↑ Pelicans, Franklin's gulls and cormorants are residents of Last Mountain Lake during the breeding season.

← The marshes of Last Mountain Lake National Wildlife Area are home to over 60 species of birds.

↓ Rare sights, endangered whooping cranes have been spotted in the area during spring and fall migrations.

# Little Manitou Lake

**Feel literally unsinkable in Canada's largest saltwater lake**

## What Makes This Hot Spot Hot?

- Little Manitou Lake is one of only three lakes in the world where the water is saturated with mineral salts.
- The water provides healing and therapeutic properties, and salts and mud from the lake are used in spa treatments.
- Nearby hiking trails connect the tranquil Wellington Park to the area's campground.

**Address:** Manitou Beach, SK
**GPS:** 51.72091; −105.44457
**Tel:** (1-866) 756-6665
**Website:** watrousmanitou.com

**Open June to August**

&#9855; (Limited, check ahead)

↗ **Floating is so easy in Canada's Dead Sea that you can read a book while taking a dip.**

Often called Canada's Dead Sea, Little Manitou Lake is found within the resort village of Manitou Beach, located between Regina and Saskatoon. Unique in the western hemisphere, the lake is known for its salinity and healing properties.

So what exactly does it mean when the water's salt levels are three times more concentrated than ocean water? Buoyancy! Those who enter the water can float with ease — lay back, read a book or visit with friends while suspended effortlessly near the surface.

As an endorheic (terminal) basin, the lake doesn't have constant flow to or from rivers and streams. It remains calm and uninterrupted for long periods, and over time the lake's salinity increases as water evaporates. The water, dense with minerals, eventually reaches a point where it can no longer hold salt in a dissolved state.

This 22.5-kilometre-long and 1.6-kilometre-wide lake has long been regarded as legendary. The lake was named *Manitou*, Algonquian for "Great Spirit," because of its mysterious qualities. Since the early 1800s, Indigenous Peoples have visited these sacred mineral-rich waters, reverent of the lake's many health benefits.

↑ **The sun sets over Little Manitou Lake.**

The lake remains a sought-after tourist destination today for the same reason. Not only is it amusing, floating effortlessly in the water, but also the minerals from the lake offer an all-natural therapeutic dipping experience that attracts visitors far and wide.

From healing sunburns to providing relief from conditions such as arthritis and psoriasis, the buoyancy of the water and its density of sodium, magnesium and potassium salts help those with chronic ailments. The water is also known to help boost the immune system and even aid in skin tightening.

Both salt and mud from Little Manitou Lake are used in spa treatments at the local Manitou Springs Resort and Mineral Spa. The lake's beneficial water can also be found in the resort's indoor mineral pools, which are open year-round.

While in the area, hike the Manitou Beach Trails. The well-groomed trails (3.5-kilometre and 5-kilometre loops) can be accessed from Manitou and District Regional Park campground and will lead you through Wellington Park, a tranquil area with a bubbling stream. There you can spot wildlife, such as mule and white-tailed deer, shorebirds and waterfowl.

# Moose Jaw

*Urban adventure and learning abounds, from birdwatching to hiking, canoeing and camping*

## What Makes This Hot Spot Hot?

- Learn about endangered burrowing owls and the grasslands ecosystem they depend on at the Saskatchewan Burrowing Owl Interpretive Centre.
- Wakamow Valley, found minutes from downtown, features 200-plus hectares of parkland and 20 kilometres of year-round trails.
- Take the city's walking tour featuring 40-plus outdoor murals.

**Address:** Moose Jaw, SK
**GPS:** 50.39393; –105.53024
**Tel:** (306) 693-8097
**Website:** tourismmoosejaw.com

**Open year-round**

&#9855; (Check ahead)

Nowhere else in the world will you be welcomed to a city by the world's tallest moose. Standing 9.8 metres high, Mac the Moose, the official greeter for Moose Jaw, is hard to miss.

Found in southcentral Saskatchewan, Moose Jaw is a city with several theories as to how exactly it got its unique name. One theory is that the name came from the shape of its river, said to look similar to a moose's jawbone. Another is attributed to Plains Cree settlers who named the area *moscâstani-sîpiy*, which translates as "a warm place by the river." The valley, shielded by the Missouri Coteau, was a settlement for both Indigenous Peoples and fur traders. The Plains Cree word *moose gaw*, meaning "warm breezes," lends itself to another theory for its unusual name.

Since the early 2000s, Moose Jaw has attracted many visitors due to the notoriety of its historic tunnels, which can be experienced via guided walking tours. Constructed in 1908 as utility tunnels through which steam engineers could access

buildings, they were once used to hide Chinese immigrant workers. Later, in the 1920s, the tunnels hosted rum-running bootleggers during U.S. Prohibition. Rumour has it that infamous mobster Al Capone visited Moose Jaw and had interest in its bootlegging operation. You can learn all about the intriguing history of the tunnels by going on "The Passage to Fortune" and "The Chicago Connection" tours run by the Tunnels of Moose Jaw.

Back above ground, the city has a couple of standout options for nature nuts. Crescent Park in the heart of the city is especially charming. Walking paths, footbridges, woodcarvings, an amphitheatre and historical buildings make it a favourite spot for locals.

Another urban park, Wakamow Valley, is found just minutes from downtown. Featuring 200 or so hectares of parkland and 20 kilometres of year-round trails, it's a natural draw for all seasons. Moose Javians (yep, that's what they're called!) enjoy their daily walks, jogs or bikes on the trails, while winter lovers appreciate the groomed

trails for cross-country skiing and snowshoeing. Seasonal camping is available, and visitors also have the option to explore the area by canoe or kayak (rentals are available from Boh's Cycle and Sporting Goods in the park).

With over 190 bird species sighted in the park, the spring season attracts birders seeking a glimpse of migrating visitors, such as olive-sided flycatchers, song sparrows and belted kingfishers. However, bird lovers shouldn't miss a visit to the Saskatchewan Burrowing Owl Interpretive Centre, which is found at the city's exhibition grounds. This site was chosen because burrowing owls are known to nest at the infield of the racetrack, and the centre offers an up-close-and-personal look at this delightful, tiny species. Informative in-house tours shed light on the ongoing conservation efforts to protect this endangered bird. You can also view a small captive population of burrowing owls in outdoor enclosures.

Also at the interpretive centre is the Evergreen Native Prairie Garden, where you can learn about the grasslands prairie ecosystem and see endemic plants, such as gaillardia, blue grama grass and prairie coneflower.

An easy and active way to learn about Moose Jaw is to take a walking tour of the city's downtown core, where over 40 giant murals depict the city's history. A list and printable map can be found at moosejaw.ca/murals.

↑ Paddlers can rent canoes and kayaks in Wakamow Valley to enjoy a day on the Moose Jaw River.

↓ Burrowing owls, whose populations are in steep decline due to habitat loss, can be viewed at the Saskatchewan Burrowing Owl Interpretive Centre.

# Moose Mountain Provincial Park

**Summer and winter outdoor lovers can choose from forests and lakes designed to suit year-round activities**

## What Makes This Hot Spot Hot?

- The park contains an extensive shared trail system of over 100 kilometres.
- Birders can hike the Beaver Lake Trail and spot mourning warblers, great-crested flycatchers and broad-winged hawks.
- A variety of fish can be found in the area, including walleye, northern pike, yellow perch, white sucker and burbot.

**Address:** Kenosee Lake, SK
**GPS:** 49.83363; –102.29551
**Tel:** (306) 577-2600
**Website:** tourismsaskatchewan.com/places-to-go

**Open year-round; camping is available May long weekend to end of October**

&#9855; (Limited, check ahead)

Positioned on a plateau, forests of poplar and birch fill out the hilly surroundings of Moose Mountain Provincial Park in the southeast corner of the province.

As one of Saskatchewan's first provincial parks, Moose Mountain is unique in that it's one of a few to have a town within the park. The resort village of Kenosee Lake has long been a go-to destination for campers (including equestrian campers) and cabin dwellers who enjoy year-round recreation.

The park has two main lakes — Little Kenosee Lake and Kenosee Lake (the park's largest body of water) — that serve as its central tourist attractions for boating, swimming and fishing. Non-motorized and close to the campgrounds, Little Kenosee Lake is the ideal place for a serene kayak or canoe excursion. A variety of fish, including walleye, northern

pike, yellow perch, white sucker and burbot, make the lake a draw for anglers as well.

The park boasts an extensive shared trail system offering over 100 kilometres of hiking and cycling trails, some of which are also used by horseback riders. Through interpretive trails and guided hikes, trail users can weave through forests of standing green ash and Manitoba maple. Watch for wildlife along the 3-kilometre White-Tailed Deer Trail, including moose, pronghorn antelope, badgers, foxes, coyotes and (surprise!) white-tailed deer, to name a few. Starting from Fish Creek Campground, this trail also features a gorgeous view of Little Kenosee Lake.

One of the park's best birding trails is the Beaver Lake Trail (4.5 kilometres), where mourning warblers, great-crested flycatchers and broad-winged hawks may be seen. Birders will want to keep their eyes peeled for the

yellow-throated vireo, which can be found on mature stands of trees on well-drained slopes, and the eastern wood pewee, often spotted near Little Kenosee Lake.

For forest views, hike the 2-kilometre Birch Forest Trail, which is found close to Kenosee Lake. While hiking, common wildflowers, such as bluebells, buttercups, golden aster, prairie roses and yellow lady's slippers, can also be seen. ATV enthusiasts are also able to enjoy designated trails between mid-June and Labour Day.

Summer is very busy in Moose Mountain, but it's also a great place to visit in the winter. Over the snowy season the same network of trails becomes groomed classic and skate cross-country skiing trails. Skiers will like the variety, as the 57 kilometres of tracks range from easy to expert. Additionally, the park becomes a haven for snow lovers of every sort, with more than 120 kilometres of groomed snowmobile trails and 10 kilometres of snowshoe trails. Families can head to the park's lookout point close to the resort for winter sliding. Toboggan Hill offers a steep and speedy descent, but little ones will find safe fun on Bunny Hill. The base of the hills features a shelter stocked with wood — perfect for warming up.

↑ The serene surroundings of Little Kenosee Lake make it perfect for canoeing.

↓ Mourning warblers are common visitors to Moose Mountain Provincial Park.

# Ravine Ecological Preserve

*A self-guided trail through a diverse environment, featuring grassland, aquatic and parkland forest habitats — all found within city limits*

## What Makes This Hot Spot Hot?

- Peace Grove features 13 spruce trees representing Canada's provinces and territories.
- An arboretum contains over 80 species of ornamental trees and shrubs.
- Waterfowl such as pintails, canvasbacks, lesser scaups, cinnamon teals, American widgeons, and buffleheads can all be spotted.

**Address:** At the corner of Sully Ave and Hwy 52, Yorkton, SK
**GPS:** 51.21138; –102.49559
**Tel:** (306) 786-1750
**Website:** yorkton.ca

**Open year-round; the trail is maintained from spring to fall**

&#9855; (Limited, check ahead)

↗ **Cinnamon teal ducks are just one of the many duck species that can be found in the preserve.**

Finding nature within the city is easy with a visit to the Ravine Ecological Preserve in Yorkton.

Found in the city's west end, mere steps from the leisure centre, this 8-hectare preserve features an arboretum and a 2.8-kilometre walking trail that loops around a pond. One trailhead can be accessed near the arboretum in the southwest corner of the park, where parking is available.

Expect to see a mixture of ecosystems as you follow the trail north. A marshy ravine turns into a landscape of aspen forest full of mature poplar, spruce, ash and willow trees and eventually morphs into open grasslands. The trail is well maintained between spring and fall. Though it isn't groomed in winter, snowshoers still use the trail.

During the warm seasons, the area is alive with the serenades of songbirds and waterfowl, such as pintails, canvasbacks, lesser scaups, cinnamon teals, American widgeons and buffleheads. Several species of mammals, reptiles and amphibians can also be found throughout the park, adding to the sense of being immersed in nature.

Flora enthusiasts will want to take their time examining and learning about the grasses, flowers and trees found here. Trees native to Saskatchewan are marked and can be viewed along the trail. Saskatoon berries, chokecherries, hazelnut, twinning honeysuckle and wood rose add pops of colour to the landscape.

The southwest corner features an arboretum, where upwards of 80 species of ornamental trees and shrubs native to the Yorkton region are grown. Search for the flowering variations of spirea (such as snow white and

bridal wreath), blue bird and Rosy O'Grady clematis and the bright yellow petals of the coronation triumph and moonlight potentilla, to name a few.

In the same area, a little "peace" can be found. A fitting place for a moment of solace, Peace Grove features a ring of 13 spruce trees representing the provinces and territories of Canada. Planted in 1992 and dedicated to supporting international peace efforts, the project is a legacy of Canada 125.

↑ **Hikers are rewarded with lovely water views along the majority of the trail.**

→ **Mature forest eventually morphs into grasslands.**

# Regina

**A nature-rich urban centre surrounded by even more outdoor opportunities**

## What Makes This Hot Spot Hot?

- In addition to hectares of parkland, Wascana Park is bursting with family-friendly recreation, from canoeing and stand-up paddleboarding to cross-country skiing.
- Bird lovers will be in their element at Wascana Marsh and A.E. Wilson Park.
- The city is close to other outdoor destinations, like the Wascana Trails, a hub for hiking and mountain biking.

**Address:** Regina, SK
**GPS:** 50.43741; –104.60927
**Tel:** (306) 789-5099
**Websites:** tourismregina.com, wascana.ca

**Open year-round**

&#x267f; (Check ahead)

Found smack dab in the centre of the continent, in southcentral Saskatchewan, is the province's capital, Regina — commonly referred to as the Queen City.

The hand planting of over 300,000 trees plus the addition of the human-made Wascana Lake changed Regina's backdrop from a relatively unremarkable plains terrain into a lovely city with an abundance of green space centered on a beautiful lake.

Today, the city is best known as home to the Royal Canadian Mounted Police and the Saskatchewan Roughriders, with their frenzied watermelon helmet–wearing fans. But it's Wascana Lake and the vast 9.3-kilometre park built around it that are undoubtedly the shining stars when it comes to outdoor experiences in the city.

Wascana Park attracts scores of residents and tourists daily. Walking, jogging and cycling the 4-kilometre loop around the lake (which extends to 6.6 kilometres if you include the marsh) are par for the course in terms of activities, as is exploring the multi-use trail system. This walking/bike path is part of the Great Trail (Trans-Canada Trail) that stretches through the park and skirts in and around the city.

The lake is also heavily used during the spring to fall months for water-based activities, such as stand-up paddleboarding, kayaking, canoeing and kite surfing. Many events take place in the park year-round, from summer dragon boat races and marathons to winter festivals and more.

Boasting lush parkland and marshland, Wascana Park attracts a good variety of birds and wildlife. Over 32 mammal species have been noted, such as foxes, weasels, beavers, bats and white-tailed jackrabbits.

With open prairie surrounding Regina, it's not uncommon to see larger wildlife roaming within city limits. Sometimes, the odd moose retreats to Wascana Lake for a dip in the water to cool off. Though Saskatchewan isn't known for turtles, the discovery of a 26.6-centimetre western painted turtle in Wascana Marsh made headlines in recent years. Olga the turtle is thought to be the largest of her species found in North America.

For fabulous birding

opportunities, bird lovers should head to Waterfowl Park, located in the 223-hectare Wascana Marsh. Display ponds (open from May to September) are home to captive and injured waterfowl. In addition to the local colonies of Canada geese, the park attracts a whole host of other birds, such as snow geese, pelicans, cormorants, finches, warblers, woodpeckers, brown thrashers and more. Part of the Wascana Lake Migratory Bird Sanctuary, this area along with Goose Island and Pelican Island provides valuable habitat for various birds, mammals, reptiles, amphibians, fish and plants.

For the relaxed birder who wants to get a good walk in while also paying attention to the tweets, hoots and hollers, Wascana Park is a great place to wander and spot at the same time. The Wascana Centre website features a bird checklist that is free to download.

If birding is your thing, also plan to check out A.E. Wilson Park. Downstream from Wascana Lake, this smaller reservoir has recorded 196 species of birds. Look for nesting orioles, warblers and flickers along with waterfowl, including avocets, loons and scoters.

Wascana Centre is just as popular in the winter, attracting those who love to play in the snow, with several kilometres of groomed cross-country ski trails (which range from

⬆ An aerial shot showcases Regina's crown jewel, Wascana Lake.

⬇ Double-crested cormorants are commonly spotted on the lake.

beginner to advanced) and toboggan runs at Douglas Park.

Just outside of the city, kite skiers take full advantage of the perfect conditions for the sport. After all, this part of the province has an abundance of flat space, snow and (usually) windy conditions that make it ideal for catching big air.

One of the best things about living in or visiting Regina is its close access to several of the province's most popular beaches and outdoor destinations. From the city it's a mere 30- to 45-minute drive to cottage and camping country.

Spots like Last Mountain Lake National Wildlife Area (page 130), Regina Beach, Buffalo Pound Provincial Park (page 108) and the Qu'Appelle Valley can be easily accessed and offer activities like water sports, fishing, hiking, birding and wildlife watching.

There are several even closer options (under 20 minutes), such as Lumsden, Craven, White Butte, Condie Marsh and Wascana Trails, where visitors can also go birding, wildlife watching, hiking, biking or cross-country skiing.

Found within the beautiful confines of the Qu'Appelle Valley, the Wascana Valley Nature Recreation Site, or the Wascana Trails as the locals refer to it, is a 15-kilometre trail system that's recognized as the main mountain biking destination in the Regina

area. One of the province's best spots for challenging bike trails, it also attracts hikers, snowshoers and cross-country skiers with its variety of trails (which range from beginner to advanced). The trails were originally developed for the 2005 Canada Summer Games and are part of the Great Trail. Thanks to its sheltered valley location and mixed grasslands, the Wascana Valley Nature Recreation Site is also a prime destination for birdwatching and wildlife viewing.

↖ **Groomed cross-country ski trails can be found throughout Wascana Centre.**

← **A.E. Wilson Park is a fantastic urban birdwatching spot.**

↑ **The Wascana Trails offers easy to advanced multi-use trails.**

→ **There are plenty of trails in and around the city for biking enthusiasts.**

# Saskatchewan Landing Provincial Park

*A historically significant river crossing, this park attracts hiking and wildlife enthusiasts, as well as cyclists and equestrians*

## What Makes This Hot Spot Hot?

- The park is one of three provincial parks in Saskatchewan to cater to equestrians.
- Visitors can find an assortment of berry bushes, such as chokecherry, Saskatoon berry, buffalo berry and hawthorn, while hiking the trails.
- Endangered birds, such as loggerhead shrikes, golden eagles, burrowing owls and ferruginous hawks, can be spotted in the park.

**Address:** Hwy 4, 50 km north of Swift Current, SK
**GPS:** 50.64716; –107.96300
**Tel:** (306) 375-5525
**Website:** tourismsaskatchewan.com/places-to-go

**Open year-round; camping is available May long weekend to Labour Day**

 (Check ahead)

Located along Highway 4, down in Stewart Valley, Saskatchewan Landing Provincial Park is a beautiful haven in the middle of the Prairies that will stop you in your tracks.

With the park straddling Lake Diefenbaker's west end, water lovers can take advantage of the kilometres of shoreline through a variety of activities, such as swimming, canoeing, kayaking, sailing and world-class fishing. On land, it's the perfect spot to immerse yourself in nature and history — on foot, on wheels or by horseback.

The park is home to a number of interpretive trails and historical sites showcasing a variety of landscapes, from native prairie terrain to forested areas, along with ravines and hills. Trembling aspen is common to the area, and other species such as hybrid poplar, Manchurian elm, green ash and caragana were all planted after the construction of the Gardiner Dam to the east.

A historically significant site, Saskatchewan Landing has been an important and

natural crossing point on the South Saskatchewan River for centuries. Learn about the history of the region at Goodwin House. Built in the late 1800s, it became a stopping point for travellers crossing the river. Today, Goodwin House doubles as the main park office and a museum featuring interpretive displays. It's open early July to Labour Day.

Hikers can trek in the footsteps of past visitors via three trails, including the historical 2.6-kilometre Rings, Ruts and Remnants Trail. Tipi rings and stone cairns, left behind from Blackfoot, Assiniboine and Plains Cree nations, among others, who once inhabited the river valley, can be viewed along the hike, as can remnants from homesteaders. The trail includes several large hills that some hikers may find challenging.

The Ridges and Ravines Trail (1.2 kilometres) and the Prairie Vista Trail (2.1 to 3.5 kilometres) explore the diversity of the prairie ecosystem. Look for berry bushes such as chokecherry, Saskatoon berry, buffalo berry and hawthorn, which can all be seen along the way.

All three trails are rich with birding and wildlife-watching opportunities. You can spot amphibians, like leopard frogs, chorus frogs and tiger salamanders, and endangered birds, such as loggerhead shrikes, golden eagles, burrowing owls and ferruginous hawks. Badgers, bobcats, foxes, pronghorn antelope and white-tailed and mule deer are also residents to look out for.

For those who like to explore on two wheels, the park features beginner to intermediate cycling routes. Though trails are not designated, horseback riders can explore several kilometres of scenic terrain on the river's south side, where they can also find a limited-service campground with corrals, tie stalls and water access.

↑ There are three trails to choose from in Saskatchewan Landing.

← Equestrians are able to explore and stay in the park at campsites that cater to riders.

↓↓ Tiger salamanders are just one of several amphibians found in the park.

↓ Looking up, you may catch a glimpse of an endangered ferruginous hawk.

# Central Saskatchewan

# Creighton Limestone Crevices

**Geological features left behind by the last ice age, these fascinating limestone crevices attract adventure seekers**

## What Makes This Hot Spot Hot?

- The limestone that forms the crevices is made from remnants of an ancient sea.
- Mycology enthusiasts will find several species of lichen in the area to admire.
- Even during the summer, snow and ice can be found at the base of the crevices.

**Address:** Hwy 167, 15 km south of Denare Beach, SK
**GPS:** 54.53909; –102.13380
**Tel:** (306) 688-8253
**Website:** townofcreighton.ca

**Open year-round**

↗ **Cup lichen can be found on tree bark or small patches of rotting wood near the crevices.**

Though this is not an official tourist site, the limestone crevices found near Creighton attract many visitors. These fascinating formations have become regional phenomena, drawing in curious adventurous types seeking an up-close look from above and within the crevices.

The crevices are located on the eastern shore of Amisk Lake, but the cliffs and their sharp edges and deep wedges are hardly noticeable until you're close enough to stare down into the gorges, so make sure you keep an eye out when approaching the crevices.

Surrounded by a green forest backdrop and covered in golden lichen, these geological features are quite remarkable. They are cracks in the Red River Formation, carbonate rock made of remnants of an ancient sea deposited on the Canadian Shield over 450 million years ago. Since the last ice age, the repeated freeze-thaw cycles have created deep fissures in the rocks, which range from 6 to 12 metres deep.

In addition to golden lichen, several other lichen species are found in the area, such as caribou and cup lichen and the green-coloured woolly foam lichen, a common species found in the boreal forest.

If you visit during midsummer, you may spot snow or ice on the moss-covered floors of the deep crevices. With the passageways so narrow and deep, oftentimes the sun's rays don't reach down far enough to melt the snow.

It's very important to note there are risks to visiting and exploring this area. There are no safety features, such as railings, in place. This spot isn't recommended for children or pets, so if you are travelling with your family or animals, take extra caution. Also ensure you take everything out that you bring into the area.

↗ **Golden lichen and moss cover the steep crevices, which descend 6 to 12 metres down.**

→ **Visitors can find the crevices along the eastern shore of Amisk Lake.**

# Crooked Bush

**Folklore drives scores of visitors each year in search of this unique cluster of crooked trees**

## What Makes This Hot Spot Hot?

- A winding boardwalk guides visitors through a grove of peculiar, crooked trembling aspen.
- Saskatchewan's largest and oldest tree, the Popoff Tree, can be found nearby.
- The Redberry Lake Migratory Bird Sanctuary, an important fall and spring staging area for migrating waterfowl, is located nearby.

**Address:** From Hafford, SK, head 14.5 km west on Hwy 40, 16 km north on Flint Rd and then 2.5 km east (watch for signs)
**GPS:** 52.8711; −107.53702
**Tel:** (306) 549-2331
**Website:** tourismsaskatchewan.com

**Open year-round**

↗ **Visitors follow the boardwalk to view this patch of twisted aspens.**

A noted botanical mystery exists a couple hours' drive from Saskatoon.

On private land northwest of the town of Hafford, in the Redberry Lake Biosphere Reserve, is a grove of trembling aspen trees that appear anything but normal. Nearly every tree on the 1-hectare grove exhibits mystic traits. Snaking, bending and intertwining instead of reaching straight upwards, the kinked trees are a natural spectacle that for a long time remained a mystery but continue to generate theories.

Scientists maintain that the peculiar tree growth is due to a mutation, though they are unsure what caused it. Paranormal folks, however, say that walking through the grove is an experience that can be felt. Some even claim to experience dizziness. Apparently cattle will not travel through the stand of atypical trees.

Weirder yet, a mere 10 metres from the grove, there are regular aspens standing straight and tall.

A curving boardwalk takes visitors through the eerie patch to admire each and every anomalous aspen. These trees reach about 4.5 to 6 metres tall and are estimated to be about 70 years old. That height is average for a 15-year-old aspen. The trees continue to grow at a normal rate, in every direction but upwards.

Plan a visit during the summer months when the trees have fully leafed out or, if you dare, in October for Halloween. When in the area, look for Saskatchewan's largest and oldest tree, the Popoff Tree. Named after Samuel J. Popoff, who once owned the land on which the tree is found, the 160-year-old cottonwood-balsam poplar hybrid stands 22 metres tall and boasts a circumference of 5 metres. It can be found south of Blaine Lake on Highway 12. Also worth a visit is the Redberry Lake Migratory Bird Sanctuary, an important spring and fall staging area for migrating waterfowl. Read more about the sanctuary on page 166.

# Greenwater Lake Provincial Park

*Located in a transition zone between boreal forest and parkland, this park is a draw for flora and fauna enthusiasts and those seeking a variety of outdoor activities*

## What Makes This Hot Spot Hot?

- The transitioning habitats within the park make it an ideal place to spot diverse animal and plant species.
- Both Highbush Interpretive Trail and Marean Lake Birding Trail are great for wildlife watching and plant scouting.
- Once thought to be extinct in Saskatchewan, trumpeter swans breed in the park.

**Address:** Hwy 38, 28 km southwest of Porcupine Plain, SK
**GPS:** 52.49149; –103.50806
**Tel:** (306) 278-3515
**Website:** tourismsaskatchewan. com/places-to-go

**Open year-round; camping is available May long weekend to Labour Day**

&#9855; (Check ahead)

Gleaning its name from its tree-filled reflective hue, Greenwater Lake Provincial Park sits on the southern end of Saskatchewan's boreal forest and northern edge of aspen parkland, a few kilometres from the town of Porcupine Plain.

The park attracts campers — mostly families — so it's no secret to those who frequent the park that it can be tough to reserve a site, as both of the park's lakes, Greenwater and Marean, are very popular.

Log cabin rentals are also steadily booked throughout the year, with the cold season drawing in anglers and adventure seekers. Many snowmobilers return each winter to whiz and wind through 100 kilometres of groomed trails. Cougar Canyon Trail is a large draw, offering a scenic vista atop a high ridge just before it descends to Big Valley Lake. Though the trail narrows, it's the 46-metre drop-off and the views that riders enjoy most. The park also features over 25 kilometres of

groomed beginner and intermediate cross-country ski trails.

During the summer, the park's beauty can be easily taken in along one of the park's two interpretive trails. Highbush Interpretive Trail and Marean Lake Birding Trail are ideal for wildlife watching and plant scouting.

Bouquets of marsh marigolds adorn the banks of Greenwater Creek along the Highbush Trail. Both deciduous and mixed-wood forests of mature trembling aspen, balsam poplar, birch and spruce are found throughout the park with an understory of alders, red osier dogwood, willows and more.

The widely used Marean Lake Birding Trail is a favourite among locals. Overlooking the lake, this wide trail features a 5.5-metre-tall viewing tower, making it a birdwatcher's best bet to see some of the 200-plus species that have been spotted in the park. Yellow-bellied

sapsuckers, common yellowthroats, ospreys, bald eagles, red-breasted mergansers and more can be found. Once thought to be extinct in Saskatchewan, as many as six pairs of trumpeter swans breed in the park, so keep an eye out. Greenwater Lake Provincial Park is one of only two areas in Saskatchewan where trumpeter swans breed.

Wildlife viewing in Greenwater Lake is different than in the south of the province. The boreal forest is home to a host of mammals, such as black bears, fishers, lynx, otters, moose and wolves.

Of course, the water is a big draw, too. The lakes are quite tranquil, so heading out on a canoe is recommended. Rainbow trout fishing at Steiestol Lake is a special feature in the park, but the usual suspects — pike, perch and walleye — can all be caught in Greenwater Lake or nearby Marean Lake.

↑ Greenwater Lake Provincial Park sits between boreal forest and aspen parkland.

← The park is one of two areas in the province where trumpeter swans breed.

↓ Look for plants and wildlife while hiking one of the park's two interpretive trails.

# Hudson Bay

**Snowmobiling may be its biggest draw, but this northcentral spot has lots to offer beyond winter sports**

## What Makes This Hot Spot Hot?

- Hudson Bay and the surrounding area have some of the province's best outdoor recreation opportunities, from snowmobiling and hiking to fishing.
- Hudson Bay has been touted the "Moose Capital of the World," as moose are commonly spotted.
- Botany enthusiasts can find the endangered ram's head lady's slipper, a rare orchid that is also the town's official flower.

**Address:** Hudson Bay, SK
**GPS:** 52.85679; –102.38811
**Tel:** (306) 865-2261
**Website:** townofhudsonbay.com

**Open year-round**

↗ **Swamp saxifrage, one of the rarest plants in the province, has been seen in the Hudson Bay area.**

If you were to name a snowmobile capital of the province, chances are it would be Hudson Bay. Beyond incredible winter offerings, however, Hudson Bay will surprise visitors no matter the season.

Found within the Red Deer Valley, among the Pasquia and Porcupine hills, is a lush area teeming with unspoiled wilderness and outdoor opportunities.

Blessed during the snowy season (November to April), with average snowfalls of nearly 2 metres, Hudson Bay boasts an astounding 680 kilometres of immaculately groomed snowmobile trails that can be directly accessed from pretty much anywhere in town. Those, along with well-maintained warm-up shelters, make it a well-loved winter playground. Nearby Wildcat Hill Provincial Park (page 174) also attracts snowmobilers who want to take advantage of great snow conditions and hundreds of kilometres of ungroomed trails. ATVs and bikes make for great ways to take in the beauty of the region during the warmer months.

As the area is surrounded by several ecological reserves, many animals enjoy this natural and protected habitat, particularly moose. Hudson Bay has been touted as the "Moose Capital of the World," so be sure to watch for these commonly spotted gentle giants. White-tailed deer, often seen grazing roadside near the forest's edge, are also found in abundance. Black bears, elk, wolves, squirrels, muskrats and beavers add to the lineup of warm-weather wildlife. Cougars and woodland caribou are occasionally sighted in the area.

You can also enjoy outstanding butterfly-watching

opportunities: look for brush-foots such as the common alpine and satyr comma. For birders, over 350 bird species can be observed in the area. Listen for the cry of the common loon, which can be heard near most local waterways. One such waterway is Ruby Lake, found in Hudson Bay Regional Park, 15 kilometres from town. This lake area is also a popular spot for swimming, sailing, windsurfing, waterskiing, wakeboarding, tubing and canoeing.

Due to its proximity to the uplands, the region is rich in native plants and rare plant species. Hudson Bay Regional Park is one of four locations in the province where you can find the rare and endangered ram's head lady's slipper, which is the town's official flower. This park also features 21 other orchid species, of which seven are endangered. Nature lovers can scour nearby Brockelbank Hill and Waskwei River areas for more uncommon plant species. Violets and plants, such as the mountain bladder fern, can be found there. Swamp saxifrage, perhaps the rarest plant in the province, has also been identified in the area, just west of town near Fir River Road.

Clear lakes, rivers and streams, along with stocked ponds, make Hudson Bay an attractive spot for anglers. Brook trout fishing can be found at Armit River and Fir River, while walleye, perch and northern pike can be caught at Helldiver Channel and Spirit, Sagnus, Townsend and Culldelsac lakes. Paddlers also enjoy the area's waterways. The Red Deer River, which flows between Hudson Bay and Red Deer Lake in Manitoba, is perfect for kayaking. Well-loved routes along the river include from Hudson Bay Regional Park to pullouts at Ridge Road (2 to 3 hours) and Erwood (7 hours).

↑ The view from Brockelbank Hill is breathtaking.

↓ The area around Hudson Bay is known for being rich in wildlife, especially moose.

# Meadow Lake Provincial Park

**With almost 1,600 square kilometres of area to explore, this boreal park is both a hiking and camping paradise**

## What Makes This Hot Spot Hot?

- Common loons, lesser scaups, otters, black bears, moose and more may be spotted along the park's many trails.
- Meadow Lake Provincial Park is home to the Boreal Trail, Saskatchewan's only destination hiking trail.
- The park features 12 additional trails that range from easy to moderately challenging.

**Address:** Hwy 4, 6 km north of Dorintosh, SK
**GPS:** 54.404432; −108.628995
**Tel:** (306) 236-7680
**Website:** tourismsaskatchewan.com/places-to-go

**Open year-round; camping is available May long weekend to Labour Day**

♿ (Check ahead)

One of Canada's largest provincial parks, Meadow Lake Provincial Park is a favourite destination for many vacationers and nature lovers alike.

With over 20 lakes, rivers and streams, along with 1,600 square kilometres to explore, the park has more than enough space to accommodate visitors. Those who come to camp love that they can choose from more than 800 sites. Featuring both front and backcountry camping, sites are spread out over 12 campgrounds.

Meadow Lake Provincial Park also has incredible beaches — some of the province's best — making water-based opportunities, such as sailing, canoeing, stand-up paddleboarding and power boating, common pastimes.

But let's get to the trails. Meadow Lake Provincial Park is an outstanding hiking destination and one of the top reasons people visit the park. Carved by ancient glaciers, the area features a wealth of lakes, lush forests and magnificent views and offers a large diversity of wildlife that can all be taken in along the trails. Be on the lookout for common loons, lesser scaups, otters, black bears, moose and more.

If you are up for it, spend a few days nature hiking along the 120-kilometre-long Boreal Trail — one of Canada's premier trails and the province's only destination hiking trail. Perfect for all levels, the well-signed and well-trodden trek showcases the beauty of the boreal forest. Hikers will make their way through stands of spruce and pine, bluffs of aspen and over slightly elevated rolling terrain, all while enjoying views of crystal-clear lakes.

You can plan single-day hikes or multi-day trips along the Boreal Trail. It has several start and end points and is connected to as many as eight front-country campgrounds and 12 backcountry campsites. Backcountry campers must pre-register.

Hikers can also choose shorter jaunts from one of 12 other trails in the park that range from easy and family friendly to moderately challenging.

Birding enthusiasts can make their way through marshy meadows and trembling aspen forests along the 4.8-kilometre Hay Meadow Hiking Trail or the 3.2-kilometre Humphrey Lake Hiking Trail. The latter follows Humphrey Lake's shoreline and eventually leads up to a viewing tower to take in a panorama.

Featuring a variety of terrain and ecosystems, the moderately difficult New Branch Hiking Trail, found between Kimball and Matheson lakes, is a 2- to 11-kilometre trail that is also great for biking. Bog cranberry, bearberry and bunchberry carpet the forest floor along the 1.8-kilometre White Birch Hiking Trail, another moderately difficult route that follows the Flotten River.

Easier loops include the Vivian Lake Hiking Trail (ranging from 1.6 to 4.2 kilometres), which takes hikers through a jack pine forest, or the easy to moderate Kimball Lake Hiking Trail (from 2 to 6.5 kilometres), which leads to Little Raspberry Lake.

Winter lovers can enjoy 20 kilometres of groomed cross-country ski trails around Greig Lake and more than 45 kilometres of groomed snowmobile trails, ranging from novice to expert, at the north shore of Kimball Lake.

↑ Spruce and pine, along with bluffs of aspen, fill out the beautiful forests of Meadow Lake Provincial Park.

↓ Otters are among the many interesting wildlife species that can be spotted in the park.

# Narrow Hills Provincial Park and the Gem Lakes

*Jewel-coloured lakes and dramatic landscapes make this a must-hike spot in the boreal forest*

## What Makes This Hot Spot Hot?

- With over 25 pristine lakes, Narrow Hills contains the greatest diversity of fish in Saskatchewan.
- Take the self-guided Narrow Hills Scenic Drive, which follows the highest ridges of the Narrow Hills.
- The 5.5-kilometre, 3-hour Gem Lakes Hiking Trail is challenging but offers spectacular views.

**Address:** Hwy 106 north of Smeaton, SK, or Hwy 120 north of Meath Park, SK
**GPS:** 54.02539; –104.6676
**Tel:** (306) 426-2622
**Website:** tourismsaskatchewan.com/places-to-go

**Open year-round; camping is available May long weekend to Labour Day**

♿ (Limited, check ahead)

With over 53,000 hectares to explore, Narrow Hills Provincial Park offers a dramatic landscape with a backdrop of hills, jack pine forests, narrow valleys and gem-coloured lakes. The knob-and-kettle terrain was formed thanks to glacial ice sheets that scoured the plains and melted, leaving behind ridges and a constellation of small deep-blue kettle lakes.

Two hours northeast of the city of Prince Albert, this park's vast wilderness area is popular among hikers and anglers.

The glacier-carved and brilliantly hued Gem Lakes are unique because no inlets to or outlets from the lakes exist. Only accumulating water from rainfall and the surrounding hills fill these sandy-bottomed, clear-watered lakes, which reflect jewel tones of jade, aqua blue and emerald and bear names like Diamond, Jade, Little Jade, Opal, Sapphire, Pearl and Little Pearl.

The best way to appreciate the lakes by land is by hiking and biking in summer and snowmobiling in winter; by water, it's on solitude-filled kayak or canoe excursions.

There are roughly 200 kilometres of hiking trails within the park. The 6-kilometre Island Lake Trail is an easy trek on sandy terrain. Moose and deer are frequently spotted along this interpretive trail, and a canopy of black spruce and jack pine tower overhead. The 5.5-kilometre, 3-hour Gem Lakes Hiking Trail is more challenging. It winds its way along lake edges and then ascends wooded ridges that offer spectacular views.

For those interested in taking a driving tour, learn about the push moraine that created the landscape 10,000 years ago along the self-guided Narrow Hills Scenic Drive. The route, which features interpretive signage, follows the highest ridges of Narrow Hills.

The park contains over 25 pristine lakes with the greatest diversity of fish in Saskatchewan — an angler's dream, especially for fly fishers. Many lakes are stocked annually with exotic trout (tiger, brown, rainbow, brook and splake). Native walleye, northern pike and perch can also be caught in the region.

With so many small, sheltered bodies of water, kayaking and canoeing are great ways to get out on the water and explore the area. Motorized boats are better suited for Zeden Lake, Lower Fishing Lake and Sealy Lake.

Campers can choose from serviced or wilderness camping. There are a handful of backcountry sites that can be accessed along the Gem Lakes Trail (Jade, Diamond and Opal lakes all offer this option). Alternatively, you can choose to rent a cabin at Caribou Creek Lodge year-round or Pine Ridge Resort in the warmer months.

↑ Biking in the park provides access to incredible vistas.

↖ Kayak or canoe along one of the area's 25 pristine lakes.

# Nipawin

**World-class fishing is what lures most folks to this area, which is sandwiched between two notable lakes**

## What Makes This Hot Spot Hot?

- Tobin Lake is home to Saskatchewan's record walleye and is one of Canada's best fishing destinations.
- Saskatoon berries, blueberries, pin cherries, chokecherries and more can be found at Nipawin and District Regional Park in the spring and summer.
- Maurice Street Wildlife Sanctuary, found just outside of town, is home to over 245 species of birds.

**Address:** Nipawin, SK
**GPS:** 53.3655; −104.01177
**Tel:** (306) 862-9866
**Website:** nipawin.com

**Open year-round**

🚶 🔭 🚴 🛶 🐎 ⛷ 🤿 ⛵
🛥 🚤 🏊 ⛺

♿ (Check ahead)

↗ **Tobin Lake is known as a world-class fishing destination.**

Nestled between two remarkable lakes — Codette Lake and Tobin Lake — Nipawin offers visitors a mix of boreal immersion and outdoor recreation opportunities.

Thanks to its lake-centric location, the area is famous for world-class fishing and recognized as one of Canada's best fishing spots. Tobin Lake is often described as the epitome of every angler's dream destination, attracting lure lovers year-round for its exceptional leisure and sport fishing both on shore and on the lake. Several tournaments are held throughout the year, and most visit with the hopes of landing a record-breaking monster-sized walleye or northern pike. In fact, the provincial record for biggest walleye has been broken four consecutive times on Tobin Lake.

Resorts, cabins and campgrounds surround Tobin Lake, and when not fishing, many take advantage of the lake for swimming, water sports and houseboating.

Codette Lake is noted as both an extraordinary fishing and recreation destination. With less traffic than Tobin, it's a better choice for those looking for a quieter angling experience while still providing access to amenities in nearby Nipawin, just 20 minutes away.

On the banks of Tobin Lake, a mere 2.5 kilometres from town, is the 120-plus-hectare Nipawin and District Regional Park. During the late spring and into the summer months, the park is nature's fruit farm, featuring tasty displays of Saskatoon berries, blueberries, pin cherries, chokecherries and more.

Nipawin also has a handful of trails both in and around the community. You can hike and bike along one of the four main trails in the area. Look for unique flowers and orchids while on the 1-kilometre Walleye Trail that winds through sand, grass and natural scrub vegetation into Nipawin and District Regional Park. Take in the town along the Central Park Walking Trail, a 2-kilometre looped hike that travels through Nipawin's beautiful 19-hectare Central Park. In the winter, there are 10 kilometres of groomed cross-country ski trails and over 300 kilometres of groomed snowmobile trails found outside of town.

Head 17 kilometres northeast of Nipawin to find thick stands of jack pine, tamarack, balsam, aspen, white spruce and more that line the trails of the Maurice Street Wildlife Sanctuary, in the heart of the boreal forest. Named a preserved sanctuary in 1968, the park gives you a chance to escape to the untamed boreal for your fill of wildlife viewing, birding and hiking. Whether looking for American redstarts and pileated woodpeckers or flowers like the ram's head lady's slipper and large yellow lady's slipper, you will enjoy spending the day out on the trails.

↑ If you're brave enough, cross the swinging bridge in Nipawin and District Regional Park.

↓ The rare ram's head lady's slipper can be spotted in Maurice Street Wildlife Sanctuary.

# Prince Albert National Park

*The meeting of lowlands and uplands provides an ecologically diverse area for those seeking a mix of wildlife watching, outdoor adventure and camping*

## What Makes This Hot Spot Hot?

- The national park is home to a protected American white pelican colony, Canada's second-largest breeding colony.
- Free-range plains bison can be spotted in the park.
- Hikers and paddlers can undertake the iconic trek to Grey Owl's Cabin.

**Address:** Waskesiu Lake, SK
**GPS:** 53.94696; –106.3888
**Tel:** (306) 663-4522
**Website:** pc.gc.ca/en/pn-np

**Open year-round**

♿ (Check ahead)

One of two national parks in Saskatchewan, Prince Albert National Park spans 3,875 square kilometres of protected land, where enchanting boreal forest meets aspen parkland. With an incredible landscape designed by ancient glaciers, the park is comprised of 30 per cent water and is rich in forests, spruce bogs and even rare fescue grassland.

It offers a good mix of accessibility and remoteness, which makes it a popular destination for those seeking active outdoor adventures. The hardest thing when visiting Prince Albert National Park is deciding what to do first.

The visitor centre, found across from the main beach area in the town of Waskesiu Lake, is open daily year-round and is the best place to gather information and make your plans. It offers plenty of cultural and nature-oriented interactive displays as well as programming to keep you busy throughout the day. Take time to visit the centre to learn about the full range of

activities in the park.

The town site of Waskesiu Lake is set within the heart of the park and attracts many who choose to stay in the area. It's an ideal hub from which to set out exploring, and it has a variety of accommodation offerings, such as camp-grounds, cabins, oTENTiks (which is a cross between a tent and a cabin) and more. For those seeking quieter areas, the park has 14 designated backcountry campgrounds.

The town also provides easy access to the lake bearing the same name and its 600-metre-long beach. This area draws scores of people who spend long summer days enjoying the beach, picnic facilities and a nearby nature-themed playground. Many visitors also partake in water sports, ranging from canoeing and kayaking to stand-up paddle-boarding, wakeboarding and waterskiing. In the winter, the lake draws adrenaline junkies for kiteskiing or kiteboarding across the icy waters. The site is perfect for both sports thanks to Saskatchewan's notoriously

fierce wind gusts.

During the summer, anglers can head to one of the three largest lakes — Crean, Kingsmere or Waskesiu — to try and reel in the area's most wanted: walleye, whitefish, suckers and northern pike. In the winter, anglers can go ice fishing on Waskesiu Lake. Ice shacks are permitted (but must be removed each night), though vehicles are not allowed on the ice. The winter season is open until March 31.

Hiking is one of Prince Albert's biggest attractions, with over 17 trails (and multiple loops within trails) spanning the park. Each of the trails possesses unique attributes, but nearly all offer breathtaking panoramas, lush vegetation and numerous

points of interest. From marshes and bogs to forested pathways and observation points, choosing even a handful of trails to explore is difficult. Whichever you choose, there are plenty of opportunities to learn about the area's ecology and spot

↑ The park is one of the only spots in Canada where plains bison still roam within their historical range.

↖ The main beach at Waskesiu Lake is a great place for families to spend the day.

↑ **Look for wildlife while hiking the 2-kilometre loop of the Mud Creek Trail.**

↗ **Outdoor adventurers can portage or hike to Grey Owl's Cabin.**

some interesting wildlife. Watch for residents such as foxes, grey wolves, moose, elk, black bears, beavers, lynx and over 200 bird species. The park protects an American white pelican colony, which happens to be Canada's second-largest breeding colony. The pelicans are found on Heron Island, on Lavallée Lake in the park's northwest corner. This area also supports large populations of nesting double-crested cormorants and ring-billed gulls.

Prince Albert National Park is also home to a herd of plains bison. In fact, it's one of the only herds in Canada that are roaming within the species' original historical range. If you come across the herd, exercise caution, and keep your distance — after all, plains bison are one of the largest land mammals in North America.

Wildlife enthusiasts should head up Narrows Road to find the Mud Creek Trail, a 2-kilometre loop where both an active beaver lodge and, thanks to spawning fish, black bears can be found. Among the loop's dark spruce and aspen stands, bird species such as warblers, hermit thrush, brown creepers and even ruffed grouse can be spotted. Many visitors enjoy the interpretive trails located a short drive from Waskesiu Lake. One favourite excursion is the Boundary Bog Trail, an easy 2-kilometre loop. This tranquil moss-covered trail features many black spruce bogs.

For the adventurous, the

park's most iconic trek, the Grey Owl Trail, provides an opportunity to hike to the cabin of Englishman Archibald Stansfeld Belaney. Belaney was a conservationist who was better known by his chosen name, Grey Owl. This 40-kilometre round-trip hike is rated intermediate and accessed through the Kingsmere day-use area. The trail follows the eastern shore of Kingsmere Lake. Hikers pass through bogs and meadows, forest and backcountry campgrounds before arriving at Grey Owl's Cabin named "Beaver Lodge," where it's rumoured he bunked with his pet beavers. Many canoeists and kayakers also portage to the cabin following the route along the eastern shoreline of the lake.

In the winter, strap on snowshoes or cross-country skis to enjoy lake views while exploring Waskesiu Lake's beach area. Prefer groomed trails? The Fisher Trail (a 6.3-kilometre loop) can be accessed from the town, or for a longer route, choose the Crean Lake Trail (which is 19 kilometres return).

Wildlife viewing in the park is optimal when it snows, as it's easy to spot fresh tracks on the roads. Drive the Narrows Road and chances are high that you'll witness elk nipping balsam buds in snowy ditches, curious grey jays flitting about and even otters venturing to and from a nearby lake.

↑ River otters call Prince Albert home year-round and are said to delight in the frigid temperatures.

↑↑ Elk are commonly spotted within the park.

# Redberry Lake Biosphere Reserve

**An ecologically significant region for many migrating bird species, this reserve promotes sustainability and conservation**

## What Makes This Hot Spot Hot?

- Redberry Lake is designated both an Important Bird Area and Migratory Bird Sanctuary.
- The reserve provides habitats for nine endangered, threatened or rare bird species, as well as over 180 other bird species.
- There are five hiking trails and plenty of recreational opportunities around Redberry Lake.

**Address:** Hwy 40, 12.8 km east of Hafford, SK
**GPS:** 52.71241; −107.21499
**Tel:** (306) 549-2360
**Website:** redberrylake.ca

**The reserve is open May long weekend to Labour Day; the regional park is open May 1 to September 30**

&#9855; (Check ahead)

The UNESCO-designated Redberry Lake Biosphere Reserve is the only one of its kind in Saskatchewan and one of just 18 designated biosphere reserves in Canada. An important conservation area, it's a wonderful place to discover native plants and animals.

Over 112,000-plus hectares of lakes, marshes, rolling hills and aspen groves make up the reserve, along with small patches of natural mixed prairie, which is rare in this part of the province. Prairie grasses, like fescue, sedge and wheat grass, can be found along with aspen and shrubs, such as gooseberry, hawthorn, raspberry, silver buffaloberry and silver willow. Lakeside in the uplands, rolling hills feature beaked hazel, dogwood, Saskatoon berry and chokecherry shrubs.

The saline Redberry Lake is a haven for birds and wildlife alike, and as a Migratory Bird Sanctuary, this area is protected. Four islands on the closed-basin, flat-bottomed lake mark an important breeding ground and staging point for both waterfowl and shorebirds. Visitors are not permitted on the islands between April 15 and September 15 so as not to disrupt nesting birds. An estimated 30,000 ducks, tundra swans and geese eat and rest here during migration seasons.

Over 180 species have been recorded, including common water-loving species (such as

American pelicans and American avocets), many types of warblers (chestnut-sided, Canada, Tennessee and more) and nine endangered, threatened or rare bird species (Sprague's pipits, loggerhead shrikes, California gulls and white-winged scoters, among others). Additionally, piping plovers nest along Redberry's sandy beaches, and the reserve is also along the migration route of one of North America's most endangered birds, the whooping crane. Fall is a great time to visit to witness the migration south as the area is quiet, although amenities are not available.

Besides birdwatching, hiking is a popular activity in the area. The intermediate 1.5-kilometre Lookout Trail features fabulous lake views, while the moderately rated 2-kilometre Grassland Golf Course Walking Trail showcases a variety of vegetation, from aspen woods to mixed grasses. An abundance of redberry bushes can be found along the easy 3.4-kilometre Millennium Point Hiking Trail, which has interpretive signage and a raised platform overlooking the marsh.

The summer months offer opportunities for swimming and water sports in Redberry Lake and fishing in the nearby trout pond, which is found in Redberry Lake Regional Park. There are 148 campsites in the regional park, and camping is available between May 1 and September 30. The quietness and remoteness of the reserve draws in cross-country skiers and snowshoers in the winter.

↑ Views of Redberry Lake.

← Listed as a vulnerable species, Sprague's pipit has been recorded in the area.

↓ Many types of warblers summer in Redberry Lake Biosphere Reserve, including the threatened Canada warbler.

# Saskatoon

**Canada's fastest-growing city, this dynamic metropolis and its surrounding areas are brimming with natural points of interest**

## What Makes This Hot Spot Hot?

- Over 80 kilometres of urban pathways can be explored along the city's Meewasin Valley Trail, found along the winding South Saskatchewan River.
- Each spring American white pelicans arriving from nesting colonies at Redberry Lake can be spotted on the river.
- Protected ecological habitats Cranberry Flats and Beaver Creek are great spots for viewing diverse flora and fauna found in the city.

**Address:** Saskatoon, SK
**GPS:** 52.12986; –106.65909
**Tel:** (1-800) 567-2444
**Website:** tourismsaskatoon.com

**Open year-round**

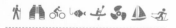

&#9855; (Check ahead)

↗ **The Prairie Lily Riverboat rests beside Saskatoon's beautiful riverfront trail.**

Straddling the South Saskatchewan River, the city of Saskatoon is divided into two sides and blends perfectly into the backdrop of aspen parkland. An anglicized version of the Cree word *misâskwatômina*, which refers to the tasty Saskatoon berry that is native to the area, Saskatoon boasts plenty of ways to explore its dynamic urban centre and the surrounding rural areas.

As riverbanks carve through the city, the Meewasin Valley Trail, found along the winding South Saskatchewan River, provides over 80 kilometres of urban waterside pathways. The trail incorporates 20 kilometres of the Trans-Canada Trail and makes exploring the city's habitats and natural sites easy. Depending on the season, locals and visitors can hike, bike, ski and kicksled along the city trails. Nearby sites of interest include the River Landing area, where a nature-themed play park makes for a fun spot for young families.

Head north along the Meewasin Trail, and you will

eventually find your way to Wanuskewin Heritage Park. Here you can learn about the culture, history and connections to the natural world of the Indigenous Peoples of the Northern Plains through outdoor experiences and indoor programming. (See page 172 for more information.)

If you head southwards on the trail, you'll run smack dab into nature at the Cranberry Flats and Beaver Creek conservation areas. These protected ecological habitats feature grasslands and are home to an abundance of native flora and wildlife. In Beaver Creek, watch for black-capped chickadees flitting and hopping near the trails.

Native fescue grassland can be found 8 kilometres northeast of downtown along the South Saskatchewan River. The Saskatoon Natural Grasslands, in the area of Silverspring, is spread out over 13.8 hectares and features a diverse ecosystem of grasses, plants and wildlife that represent over 10,000 years of natural history, since the end of the last ice age. Here you will find

↑ **Discover grassland habitats in the city at the Cranberry Flats Conservation Area.**

↑ **American white pelicans arrive in the city each spring, often landing on the South Saskatchewan River.**

a variety of wildflowers, such as the smooth goosefoot, and grassland birds, like the at-risk common nighthawk, which nests in the area.

The South Saskatchewan River offers multiple ways to take in views of the city and be active while doing so. Popular activities include windsurfing, kayaking, canoeing, powerboating or stand-up paddleboarding on the river. Alternatively, a riverboat cruise aboard the Prairie Lily is a great way to learn a little

history while admiring the views. While on board, keep your eyes peeled for American white pelicans, which are often spotted between the Canadian Pacific Railway bridge and the weir. Every spring, the once-endangered species arrives on the river, likely coming from nesting colonies at Redberry Lake. To mark their arrival and celebrate the return of spring, the Meewasin Valley Authority holds an annual Pelican Watch contest in which participants guess

the arrival time of the first pelican. A not-to-be-missed summer festival is the week-long Nature City Festival that takes place annually in May and features over 50 events focused on urban nature.

In addition to numerous festivals celebrating the winter season, there is an abundance of activities available during the cold months — from cross-country skiing in Kinsmen Park or along the Meewasin Trail (trails are maintained along both the east and west banks) to skating downtown and ice fishing at nearby lakes. For tobogganing, head to Diefen-baker Park or Pest Hill.

# Wanuskewin Heritage Park

*Impactful, authentic cultural experiences can be found at this Indigenous meeting place, where visitors can connect with nature*

## What Makes This Hot Spot Hot?

- Wanuskewin is Canada's longest-running archaeological dig site.
- Four interpretive trails allow hikers to experience both the cultural and natural wonders of the area.
- Visitors can enjoy a tipi sleepover and engaging workshops while learning all about traditional Indigenous living.

**Address:** RR #4, Penner Road, Saskatoon, SK
**GPS:** 52.22427; –106.59605
**Tel:** (306) 931-6767
**Website:** wanuskewin.com

**Open year-round**

🚶 👓 🎿

♿ (Check ahead)

↗ **Explore the mixed-grassland region surrounding Wanuskewin Heritage Park.**

You don't always have to go far to discover something new, or in this case something very old. By travelling a mere 5 kilometres outside of Saskatoon's city limits, visitors will be transported to a place where connectivity with nature and immersion in Indigenous history and culture go hand in hand.

It is estimated that humans have been gathering at Wanuskewin for the past 6,000 years. This spot was likely chosen by Northern Plains Peoples because of its topography. It is quite different than surrounding areas — with steep cliffs for buffalo jumps,

access to water and shelter from the prairie wind. Archaeological digs have been taking place on the park's site since the 1980s. This excavation project is led by the park's founder, Dr. Ernie Walker, and is the longest-running continuous dig site in Canada.

The park features 19 pre-contact sites, including two buffalo jumps. Bones and artifacts found here are thousands of years old, with many of the archaeological finds pre-dating Egypt's pyramids. During the spring and summer months, visitors can take part in tours and witness active excavations. Guided digs take

place Saturdays and Sundays in May and June and seven days a week during July and August. The park also showcases medicine wheels, tipi rings and more, uncovering the day-to-day traditions of the Northern Plains Peoples.

Wanuskewin is set above the Opimihaw Creek and South Saskatchewan River, in a moist mixed-grassland ecoregion. You can best explore the area by walking in the footsteps of ancient ancestors along four pathways and 6 kilometres of trails. Weaving through the prairie backdrop, the trails are available for exploration during any season. Keep an

eye out because there are over 100 species of birds and wildlife, such as beavers, coyotes, foxes and rabbits.

The park's evolving programming is a rich way for visitors to discover. In addition to hiking, activities such as tipi building, traditional games, workshops, crafts and dance performances help you connect with both the natural and cultural past as well as the present environment.

Wanuskewin, designated a National Historic Site in 1986, has made the UNESCO World Heritage Site tentative list and hopes to become the first World Heritage Site in Saskatchewan.

↑ A trio of bronze bison greet visitors near the front entrance. Two buffalo jumps have been discovered on the park's site.

# Wildcat Hill Provincial Park

**Experienced adventurers can truly carve their own paths in this remote park**

## What Makes This Hot Spot Hot?

- This is exclusively a "pack in–pack out" park.
- The park covers nearly 22,000 hectares and features forest, fast-flowing rivers, creek crossings, muskeg, black spruce bogs and canyons.
- Rare plant species, as well as a variety of wildlife, can be found in the park and surrounding areas.

**Address:** 40 km north of Hudson Bay, SK
**GPS:** 53.27096; –102.49523
**Tel:** (306) 278-3515
**Website:** townofhudsonbay.com

**Open year-round; park is non-operational with no facilities**

↗ The dragon's mouth orchid is considered rare in Saskatchewan.

L argely untouched and undeveloped, Wildcat Hill Provincial Park is where you can find undisturbed natural beauty and true adventure. The only catch? You must have wilderness experience to explore the area; there are no services in the park, and you have to hike in to access it. Now those might be reasons enough to stop reading here. However, if you aspire to be or already consider yourself a competent backcountry camper who can master a map and compass, read on.

Located approximately 40 kilometres north of Hudson Bay and perched high on the Pasquia Hills, Wildcat Hill Provincial Park features dense forests of tamarack and black spruce that tower over the surrounding lowlands.

This pack in–pack out park doesn't have any formed trails, with the exception of snowmobile trails during the winter months. Like Hudson Bay, Wildcat Hill is a popular snowmobiling destination with both groomed and unmaintained trails. Snowmobiling in is by far the easiest way to reach the park's interior. Accessing even the perimeter of the park's boundary during the spring, summer and fall isn't easy, as it requires a demanding hike through rugged, dense bush and forest.

So why would anyone want to visit? The chance to experience seclusion, solace and nature's beauty drives some visitors, while the challenge of true adventure and discovery entices others. Wildcat Hill has an elevation of over 670 metres and encompasses nearly 22,000 hectares of forest, fast-flowing rivers, creek crossings, muskeg, black spruce bogs, canyons and diverse wildlife. Common animal species include moose and white-tailed deer, which

migrate to the park's lower slopes during the winter. Black bears, wolves, coyotes and the occasional cougar have also been spotted in the park.

Thanks to its uplands location, rare flora can be found here. The area around Fir River Road (which is not maintained) and Highway 9 is said to be rich in rare plant species, such as the dragon's mouth orchid and large yellow lady's slipper.

Before heading to Wildcat Hills, it is recommended that you contact conservation officers at the Saskatchewan Environment Office in Hudson Bay. Detailed maps can also be obtained in Regina by calling (306) 787-2799.

↑ **Exploring Wildcat Hills is done easiest by snowmobile in the winter.**

↖ **The park is home to a variety of wildlife including black bears, moose and wolves.**

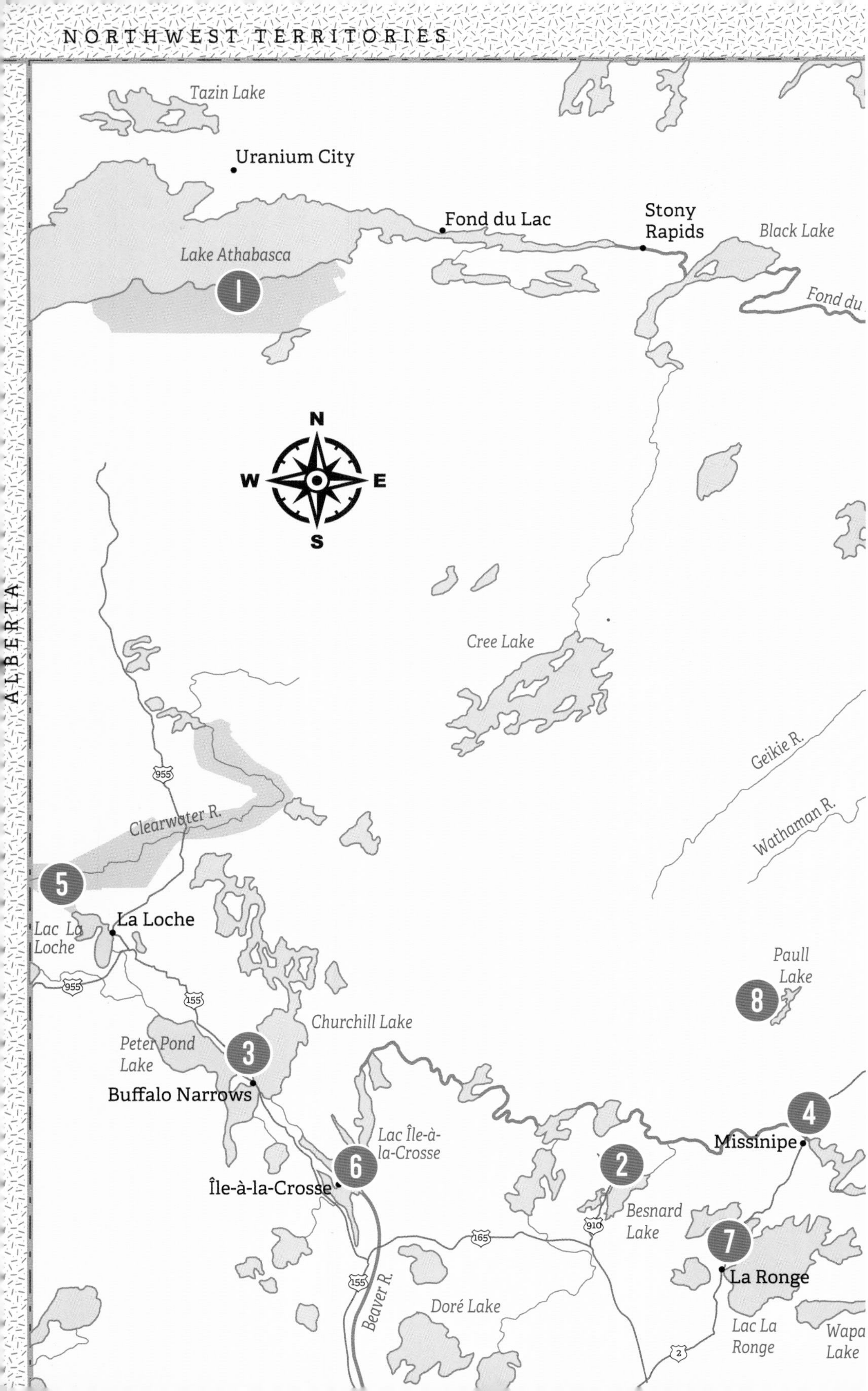

ALBERTA

Tazin Lake

Uranium City

Fond du Lac

Stony Rapids

Black Lake

Lake Athabasca

Fond du

1

N
W E
S

Cree Lake

Geikie R.

Wathaman R.

Clearwater R.

5

La Loche

Lac La Loche

Paull Lake

8

955

155

Churchill Lake

Peter Pond Lake

3

Buffalo Narrows

Lac Île-à-la-Crosse

Missinipe

4

6

Île-à-la-Crosse

2

910

Besnard Lake

7

La Ronge

165

Beaver R.

155

Doré Lake

Lac La Ronge

Wapa Lake

2

# Northern Saskatchewan

ATHABASCA SAND DUNES PROVINCIAL PARK

# Athabasca Sand Dunes

*Boreal forest meets desert-like sand dunes to form one of Canada's most unlikely and unique landscapes*

## What Makes This Hot Spot Hot?

- This is the world's most northerly sand dune formation.
- The park covers over 1,925 square kilometres and is home to over 50 rare plant species and 10 endemic plant species.
- Lake Athabasca is the largest lake in Saskatchewan and the 20th-largest lake in the world.

**Address:** There is no direct road access into the park. To fly in, make arrangements with outfitters or air charter companies that service northern Saskatchewan.
**GPS:** 59.04684; –108.8236
**Tel:** (1-800) 205-7070
**Website:** tourismsaskatchewan. com/places-to-go

**Open year-round; wilderness camping is available May long weekend to Labour Day; park is non-operational with no facilities**

↗ **The massive dunes cover over 30,000 hectares.**

Mountains of sand flowing out of the boreal forest make the Athabasca Sand Dunes one of the most unique and unexpected land features in Canada. As a pack in–pack out destination with no facilities, services and roads into it, it's not the easiest place to visit. However, for good reasons, it tops many trip wish lists.

This fragile environment, protected by the creation of the Athabasca Sand Dunes Provincial Park in 1992, is truly exceptional. Found in an ultra-remote expanse in the province's northwest, these 30,000 hectares of sandy wilderness encompass the largest set of active sand dunes in Canada and is the most northerly sand surface on the planet.

The dunes started life as a delta in a large freshwater lake. The delta was formed when glaciers melted and deposited huge amounts of sand and silt into Lake Athabasca. Over time, the lake's water levels dropped, revealing massive sand deposits. Some of the wind-sculpted ridges and hills tower over 30 metres in height.

For an area covered in sand, the diversity of plant life is surprising. Flora thrives thanks to the subarctic forest's rockbound soil, which provides ideal conditions for plant root systems to spread. There are over 300 plant species found in the wilderness park, of which

50 are considered rare and 10 endemic — in other words, not found anywhere else in the world. The large-headed woolly yarrow, felt-leaf willow, Athabasca thrift, Mackenzie hairgrass and sand stitchwort are a few of the endemics. The rarest is the impoverished pinweed, a plant with multiple stems that extend outwards from a single taproot.

The dunes are home to several mammals, such as moose, wolves, bears, martens and caribou. It's also a bird-watching mecca — 30 species of wood warblers have been spotted here.

Lake Athabasca is noteworthy as well. At 7,850 square kilometres and with a maximum depth of 124 metres, it's the largest lake in Saskatchewan and the 20th-largest lake in the world.

Access to the park is by float plane or boat. The park is recommended for visitors with wilderness experience, though guided tours are available. The best time to visit is between June and August.

You must check in with a conservation officer prior to visiting. As the park and its ecosystem are delicate, visitors are urged to avoid exploring or camping in off-limit areas, such as on the desert pavement, a layer of worn pebbles that sits atop the sands, appearing as a walkway through the dunes. Please only set up in one of the six designated, primitive campsites.

↑ Mackenzie hairgrass is one of 10 endemic plant species found in the park.

↖ It's no mirage — in this provincial park, an unlikely pairing of water and desert-like sand dunes occurs.

# Besnard Lake

**This "Lake of Many Islands" is known for its easy accessibility to rich recreational fishing opportunities and its many bald eagles**

## What Makes This Hot Spot Hot?

- Most visit the lake for fishing walleye and northern pike.
- There are over 250 islands in the area.
- Besnard Lake has long been studied for its high density of bald eagles.

**Address:** Hwy 910, west of La Ronge, SK
**GPS:** 55.41069; –106.02321
**Tel:** n/a
**Website:** tourismsaskatchewan.com

**Many outfitters are open mid-May to the end of September**

&#9855; (Limited, check ahead)

↗ **Walleye and northern pike are two species caught at the lake.**

Recreational fishing lures most visitors to Besnard Lake, found west of La Ronge, where boreal forest meets the Canadian Shield. Fed mainly by the Mercer River, Besnard Lake is the spawning area for walleye in the waters that flow north and east and form part of the Churchill River System.

Exploring the lake's 250 islands and over 140 kilometres of shoreline while spending the day trying to catch healthy-sized walleye and northern pike is how most visitors unwind. But what makes the fishing at Besnard Lake so special?

Besides being more accessible than other northern fishing spots, the lake provides anglers the chance to fish in a variety of areas, from coves and bays to deep water. Smaller islands that dot the lake double as fishing nurseries, which in turn attract larger fish.

Thanks to the abundance of fish, the area is home to a healthy population of bald eagles — so healthy, in fact, that the world's longest-running study of a stable raptor population has been ongoing in the area since 1968. The study monitors the abundance of nesting bald eagles found on the northern

part of the lake within the mixed-wood boreal forest and peatlands, where sturdy white spruce make the perfect bases for nests. This area has long held a steady population of approximately 100 bald eagles, and one of the study's key observations is that there is a higher density of adults versus juveniles. Research indicates that there's a limit on how many bald eagles can thrive in the area; therefore juveniles are pushed out. It's been noted that some of the banded adults have held off breeding until they are older (6-plus years old) in order to find suitable territory. The study has also

taught scientists how to distinguish the gender of bald eagles, which can be done by measuring the length of the pad on the talon and the depth of the beak while young eagles are still in the nest.

You can travel to Besnard Lake by either road or air. It's recommended that visitors, especially newcomers, should visit the area with a partner or ensure they have guidance from an outfitter, as the lake is very complex. There are several fishing and camping outfitters on the lake that offer accommodations, from backcountry camping to fully equipped cabins.

↑ Most people visit beautiful Besnard Lake to spend their days on the water.

↓ The area's thriving fish population accounts for the stability of the bald eagle population at Besnard Lake, the subject of a 50-plus-year study.

# Buffalo Narrows

**Surrounded by lakes, this northern community is a major recreational centre in the remote north**

## What Makes This Hot Spot Hot?

- With waterways all around, Buffalo Narrows is a popular spot for recreational fishing.
- Endangered piping plovers nest on Big Buffalo Beach.
- Wild sarsaparilla, pink lady's slipper, bearberry, starflower and more can be found in the area.

**Address:** Buffalo Narrows, SK
**GPS:** 55.86349; –108.48053
**Tel:** (306) 235-4593
**Website:** buffalonarrows.com

**Open year-round**

&#9855; (Limited, check ahead)

↗ **The ovenbird is a common species of small songbird that's often spotted in Buffalo Narrows.**

Found in the "narrows" between Churchill and Peter Pond lakes, amid the Canadian Shield and boreal forest, Buffalo Narrows was once a bison hunting ground and a departure point along the fur trade route. Today, this community, which is surrounded by waterways, bays and islands, serves as a recreation and fishing hot spot.

Peter Pond Lake is the long glacial body of water to the west. Once known as Buffalo Lake, it's technically two lakes: the larger one to the north is fittingly named Big Peter Pond Lake, and the smaller one to the south is Little Peter Pond Lake.

Directly accessed from Buffalo Narrows, Little Peter Pond Lake is a reliable fishing destination, especially during May, June and the first part of July. After that, the fish migrate to Big Peter Pond Lake, making the fishing up there from mid-July to August exceptional. Fish species found in these lakes include walleye, yellow perch, northern pike, lake trout and lake whitefish, to name a few. You can find a number of fishing outfitters in the Buffalo Narrows area.

Ice fishing is a popular winter pastime, too. Anglers who come to ice fish Peter

Pond Lake for a week during the winter have no problems catching their annual limits. To catch walleye and pike, many anglers advise using a jig at depths of between 6 and 7.5 metres.

Other recreational opportunities exist 5 kilometres north of town in Buffalo Narrows Sand Dunes Park. Covering 3,650 hectares, including the peninsula that nearly splits Peter Pond Lake, the park is a great place for nature lovers. Wander along 10 kilometres of soft white sand on Big Buffalo Beach, where you can pick wild berries along the way. Break out the binoculars to spot birds, such as ovenbirds, black and white warblers, great blue herons, greater yellowlegs and spotted sandpipers. The beach is also a known nesting site for the endangered piping plover, which typically lays its eggs in May. A variety of interesting flora can be found in the park, such as wild sarsaparilla, pink lady's slipper, bearberry and starflower.

Also found just outside town are the Waskawîhew Trails, a 13-kilometre network of trails where summer visitors can hike and bike. In the winter, the trails transform into perfect pathways for cross-country skiing.

# Churchill River

**This historic waterway stretches over 1,600 kilometres across the Canadian Shield, flowing eastwardly from Alberta all the way to the Hudson Bay**

## What Makes This Hot Spot Hot?

- Precambrian granite outcroppings and beautiful boreal wilderness surround paddlers all along this historic river.
- The river has route options for all paddlers.
- There are many points of interest, including wildlife, breathtaking waterfalls and ancient pictographs.

**Address:** Easy access to the river at Missinipe, SK
**GPS:** n/a
**Tel:** (1-877) 237-2273
**Websites:** tourismsaskatchewan.com, myccr.com/canoeroutes/saskatchewan

**Open year-round; opening times for campsites and lodges along the river will vary, so check ahead**

↗ **Ancient Indigenous pictographs can be found in a number of areas along the river.**

The Churchill River is the ultimate hot spot in the province for those who travel to paddle. The river stretches over 1,600 kilometres across the Canadian Shield, flowing eastwardly from Alberta across the northcentral part of Saskatchewan, all the way to the Hudson Bay at Churchill, Manitoba. A 487-kilometre-long section of the Churchill River between Île-à-la-Crosse on Lac Île-à-la-Crosse and Frog Portage on Trade Lake has been nominated as a Canadian Heritage River.

The Cree name for the river is *Missinipi*, meaning "big river." It couldn't ring truer. The river is a labyrinth of pristine paddling pathways connected by rapids and falls, surrounded by Precambrian granite outcroppings and beautiful boreal wilderness.

It's also steeped in history. The river was named for John Churchill, first Duke of Marlborough and the governor of the Hudson's Bay Company from 1685 to 1691. Paddlers can weave their way through history, retracing the routes of this water highway once heavily used by Indigenous Peoples and, later, European voyageurs.

The Churchill has a variety of waterways to explore, with everything from stretches of smooth water to whitewater rapids and falls. There are numerous routes and options for all levels of paddlers. The easiest way to pick a route that's right for you is to contact a local outfitter or visit the Canadian Canoe Routes website (myccr.com) for a complete list of documented routes, maps and helpful instructions.

You can also read about more specific stretches of the Churchill River in the Paull River (page 192), Clearwater River Provincial Park (page 186) and Lac La Ronge Provincial Park (page 190) sections of this book.

Pack your rod and reel, as fishing is a great activity between paddling. Try your hand at catching northern pike, walleye and sauger. Mid-May to early July is the best time to fish the waterway. While on the river, look for wildlife, like black bears, otters and beavers. Birds are also frequently spotted, including bald eagles, common loons and a variety of owls.

Several points of interest can be found along the river, such as Twin Falls, Robertson Falls and Nistowiak Falls. If you find yourself near Rattler Bay, be sure to look up at the rocks that line the shore, as ancient pictographs can be spotted.

You can easily access the river via the town of Missinipe, which is 78 kilometres north of La Ronge. Several outfitters there provide guided paddling tours in the area, which is great for beginners looking to dip their paddles into this phenomenal waterway.

↑ Take in the magnificent Canadian Shield along the Churchill River.

↖ Otter Lake is one of many lakes that are part of the Churchill River system.

# Clearwater River Provincial Park

*A paddler's paradise, where wilderness camping and canoeing in an unspoiled area meets every type of river condition*

## What Makes This Hot Spot Hot?

- Clearwater River is Saskatchewan's first Canadian Heritage River.
- The river is great for experienced paddlers, with rapids ranging from Class II to Class IV.
- The historic Methye Portage doubles as a hiking trail along which visitors can camp.

**Address:** Hwy 955, 60 km northeast of La Loche, SK
**GPS:** 56.89265; −108.9806
**Tel:** (306) 236-7672
**Websites:** tourismsaskatchewan.com/ places-to-go, myccr.com/ canoeroutes/saskatchewan

**Open year-round; wilderness camping is available May long weekend to Labour Day; park is non-operational with no facilities**

The area of Clearwater River Provincial Park, found in the province's northwest corner, encompasses most of its namesake river, which is as pristine as its name suggests. Flowing westward from northern headwaters in Broach Lake to Alberta's Athabasca River near Fort McMurray, the remote 295-kilometre-long Clearwater River is an outstanding canoeing and kayaking destination recommended for experienced paddlers.

This waterway is challenging to explore thanks to its variety. The river passes through two geological areas and features whitewater rapids that range from Class II to Class IV, along with narrow channels, broad sections, islands, sandbars, gorges snaking through limestone, waterfalls and jack pine and aspen forests. Clearwater River was designated Saskatchewan's first Canadian Heritage River in 1986. Canadian Canoe Routes (myccr. com) has an online database of documented canoe routes in Saskatchewan, and routes

40 and 58 feature stretches of Clearwater River.

It also features Northern Saskatchewan's most historic (and longest) portage: the Methye Portage between Lac La Loche and Clearwater River. With assistance from Dene Nations guides, explorer Peter Pond crossed the 20-kilometre portage in 1778, opening the region up to direct overland trade by establishing a route that would be used for the following four decades by explorers and traders. The Methye Portage was declared a National Historic Site in 1933, and it currently doubles as a hiking trail from the north end of Lac La Loche to Clear-water River.

Beyond the appeal of the river, the remote, natural and unspoiled beauty of this pack in–pack out wilderness area is ripe for exploration. Backcountry campers can set up both by the riverside and along the Methye Portage. The northwest portion of the river has fantastic northern fishing, with species like walleye, lake trout, yellow perch, northern pike, white sucker, longnose sucker, burbot and even Arctic grayling.

In the upper portion of Clearwater River, between Lloyd Lake and Careen Lake, three important Indigenous pictographs can be found. These sites are the farthest north and west that picto-graphs have been documented in the province to date.

↑ **Clearwater River runs through the stunning Skull Canyon, a perfect place to pause and take photos.**

← **The river features a variety of rapids ranging from Class II to Class IV.**

# Île-à-la-Crosse

**_Steeped in Canadian history, this northern community is also a haven for nature and recreation enthusiasts_**

## What Makes This Hot Spot Hot?

- The second-oldest community in the province, Île-à-la-Crosse was designated a National Historic Site in 1954.
- The area is replete with recreational opportunities, from paddling to foraging.
- The shore is an ideal place to spot wildlife, such as moose, black bears, beavers, muskrats and otters.

**Address:** Île-à-la-Crosse, SK
**GPS:** 55.43698; –107.89838
**Tel:** (306) 833-2122
**Website:** sakitawak.ca

**Open year-round**

&#9851; (Limited, check ahead)

⌃ **Kayaking is a good way to spend the day in Île-à-la-Crosse, which is surrounded by water.**

Touted as the North's best kept secret, the Métis community of Île-à-la-Crosse or Sakitawak, Cree for "where the rivers flow out," is the second-oldest community in Saskatchewan, established in 1776. Named a National Historic Site in 1954, the town has a deep history in the fur trade. In 1799, the Hudson's Bay Company established its first regional headquarters in the community, and five of 16 known important archaeological sites in the area are historic fur-trading posts. Île-à-la-Crosse is also the birthplace of Louis Riel Senior.

Île-à-la-Crosse is located on a peninsula that stretches into a part of the great Churchill River known as Lac Île-à-la-Crosse. The area is rich in beauty — its northern forest backdrop of tamarack, birch, poplar and jack pine trees is complemented by an abundance of rivers, lakes and streams. Plenty of wildlife can be spotted in the area. Watch the shorelines for fauna, such as moose, black bears, beavers, muskrats and otters.

The beach and lake areas are the main spots where visitors flock, with many choosing to spend their days boating or retracing historic canoe routes along the Churchill. Fishing

is by far the most popular activity with locals who love to angle during the summer as well as the winter months, when the lakes freeze over. Commonly caught species include northern pike, yellow perch, burbot and whitefish.

Looking for edible flora is another way to explore (and indulge in) the area. Just 2 kilometres outside of town at McKay Point and Favel's Ranch Area, you can forage for Labrador tea and wild berries, such as Saskatoon berries, pin cherries, cranberries, blueberries and raspberries. Berries can also be found at the South Bay War Veterans'

Park. The park, which offers camping between mid-May and mid-September, is found 3 kilometres by boat or 32 kilometres by car off Highway 155. It was also a significant fur trade hub at one time.

Winter lovers will find cross-country ski trails on Favel's Ranch Road, and families can spend a day in the snow tobogganing the hills of McKay Point.

↑ **The beach area is a great place to take in a stunning Saskatchewan sunset.**

→ **While hiking, visitors can forage for Labrador tea and wild berries.**

# Lac La Ronge Provincial Park

**One of Saskatchewan's largest, this provincial park contains over 100 freshwater lakes, historic water routes, rapids, falls and sand cliffs**

## What Makes This Hot Spot Hot?

- Lac La Ronge Provincial Park features one of the province's largest waterfalls, Nistowiak Falls.
- The park is a paddler's paradise, with over 30 documented canoe routes and whitewater rafting opportunities.
- The nearby Nipekamew Sand Cliffs are the eroded remnants of a prehistoric river.

**Address:** Adjacent to the town of La Ronge, SK
**GPS:** 55.07127; –105.3072
**Tel:** (306) 425-4234
**Websites:** tourismsaskatchewan.com/places-to-go, myccr.com/canoeroutes/saskatchewan

**Open year-round; camping is available from May long weekend to Labour Day**

&#9683; (Limited, check ahead)

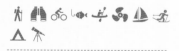

↗ **Watch for wildlife along the trails, including lynx, bears and moose.**

A tenth of Saskatchewan's lakes can be found in this provincial park, which is tucked into the Churchill River System. Lac La Ronge Provincial Park and the province's fourth-largest lake, Lac La Ronge, also encompass more than 1,300 islands.

Water is undoubtedly the shining feature in the park and can be enjoyed in multiple ways. Take in Nistowiak Falls, one of the province's largest waterfalls with a 10-metre drop. You can find the falls near the community of Stanley Mission, where Lac La Ronge joins the Churchill River.

Just outside of the northern hub of La Ronge, the park, with its historic waterways and rocky landscapes, can be explored the same way an early fur trader would — via one of 30 documented canoe routes, which can be found online on the Canadian Canoe Routes website (myccr.com). A section of route 11 from Stanley Mission to Nistowiak Falls is a popular journey that is suitable for beginners and only has one portage, at Stanley Rapids. For those seeking a fast-paced

adventure, challenging Class III rapids fit for whitewater rafting can be found at Otter Rapids on the Churchill River, north of Missinipe.

With all that water, it's not surprising that fishing is also a popular park activity. Home to Arctic grayling, rainbow trout, northern pike, walleye and more, Lac La Ronge Provincial Park attracts anglers year-round for fly-fishing, fly-in fishing and ice fishing.

The park also provides many reasons to move off the water and enjoy the Canadian Shield's beautiful surroundings on foot. The well-trodden Nut Point

Trail is a 30-kilometre round-trip trail extending along Nut Point peninsula. Hikers are rewarded with water views on both sides of the trail for the majority of the trek. Expect to climb rocky outcrops and meander over mossy forest floors and muskeg. Colourful mushrooms and a bounty of wild blueberry bushes are found alongside the trail. And where there are berries, there are often bears. Other area wildlife includes lynx, beavers, moose, ospreys, bald eagles and white pelicans.

Winter is a great time to visit, as the park features over 60 kilometres of groomed classic and freestyle cross-country ski trails and 5 kilometres of lit trails for night skiing.

A nearby feature not to be missed is Nipekamew Sand Cliffs. The cliffs are found

outside of the park, about half an hour southeast of La Ronge. These unique and fragile geological formations are remnants of an ancient river that pre-dates the last ice age. After millions of years of erosion, the vertical cliffs, which were the sands of the prehistoric river, are now exposed.

↑ The Nipekamew Sand Cliffs are fragile geological formations, the remnants of an ancient river.

↖ With over 1,300 islands in the park, water activities, such as kayaking and canoeing, are popular.

# Paull River

## *Take an epic canoe journey, or spend days casting away at this fly-in fishing hot spot*

### What Makes This Hot Spot Hot?

- This remote river is accessible thanks to a number of outfitters that offer guided fishing and paddling trips.
- Exploring this waterway gives visitors a chance to experience the natural beauty and history of northern Saskatchewan.
- Bald eagles, pelicans and loons are commonly spotted on the river, along with bears and moose.

**Address:** There is no direct road access to the river. To fly in, make arrangements with outfitters or air charter companies that service northern Saskatchewan
**GPS:** 56.1117; −104.8562
**Tel:** (1-877) 237-2273
**Websites:** tourismsaskatchewan.com, myccr.com/canoeroutes/saskatchewan

**Open year-round**

Fly-in fishing is a massive draw to Saskatchewan's north, and it's no surprise that there is a healthy offering of outfitters and lodges to help visitors explore this remote region. The area around Paull River, which winds through the country's Canadian Shield, is no exception.

Most folks go to the Paull River to get away from it all, usually by float plane directly from Missinipe. A peaceful day spent jigging on the boat for walleye or casting for northern pike followed by a shore lunch is generally par for the course. By choosing a guided adventure, you will be able to find the best fishing holes. Tuck Falls and Whitefish Lake are known to be decent spots for luring walleye.

Not everyone comes for the fishing, however.

This pristine northern wilderness can also be experienced by canoe. Venturing down routes that have been used for centuries by Indigenous Peoples, traders and other northern folk is one of the best ways to take in an area that is nearly all lakes and trees.

The Paull River is a small tributary of the Churchill River with headwaters in Paull Lake. A suggested course

is the 85-kilometre route 36, which you can find online on the Canadian Canoe Routes website (myccr.com). This route starts from Paull Lake and takes paddlers along the Paull and Churchill rivers to the town of Missinipe on Otter Lake. This journey, which takes about a week at a relaxed pace, offers paddlers a typical pool and drop flow — flat lake paddling along with brief stretches of rapids and falls. You will enjoy picturesque panoramas, dense boreal forests full of black spruce and aspen, rocky outcroppings, gorges, scenic waterfalls and whitewater, too.

Paddlers should have beginner to intermediate whitewater skills, as there are short stretches of rapids that must be run. Wilderness camping is done along the river or in any suitable location found along the way.

Bald eagles are common in the area, as are American white pelicans and common loons. Black bears and moose are also seen along the shore.

To experience some of the Indigenous history in the area, head towards Hickson Lake, where you will find ochre-painted pictographs in the channel between Maribelli and Hickson lakes.

↑ **Pristine northern wilderness surrounds the Paull River.**

↖ **Paddlers can travel historic waterways once used by northern voyageurs and fur traders.**

# Special Interest

# Birdwatching

↑ **You can find both great blue herons and great egrets in the Quill Lakes area.**

Birdwatching in Saskatchewan is a year-round experience, with the province being home to numerous staging areas and nesting sites. An influx of feathered visitors — from shorebirds and songbirds to throngs of migrating waterfowl — arrive each year, complementing the permanent residents, such as snowy owls, snow buntings and more.

Diverse ecozones and microenvironments make the province an ideal place for over 350 bird species. Saskatchewan is also home to several migratory bird sanctuaries and over 50 designated Important Bird Areas, making birdwatching an activity that can be done virtually anywhere in the province.

The northern part of Saskatchewan, within the mixed-wood boreal forest, is one of the most diverse areas in North America for bird species. In the region where the boreal forest transitions into aspens and grasslands, twitchers can spot tree dwellers, such as the

Connecticut warbler, black-backed woodpecker, great grey owl and boreal chickadee. The south is home to rolling grasslands, valleys and lakes that also offer an amazing selection of bird species. Many birding destinations are already noted in other chapters, including **Grasslands National Park** (page 120), **Last Mountain Lake** (page 130), **Buffalo Pound Provincial Park** (page 108) and **Chaplin Lake** (page 110). Here are a few more outstanding birding hot spots.

## Quill Lakes

Quill Lakes has much to offer birdwatchers. The region was acknowledged as Saskatchewan's first Important Bird Area, and like Chaplin it is recognized internationally as a birdwatching destination. This aspen parkland area north of Wynyard hosts over 300 species numbering upwards of a million visiting birds each year.

Made up of three very shallow saltwater lakes (Big Quill Lake, Mud Lake and Little Quill Lake), Quill Lakes sees an incredible number of waterfowl, making it the place to be for spring and fall migrations. Expect to spot hundreds of thousands of shorebirds, ducks, snow geese and Canada geese. Other commonly spotted birds include American avocets, black-crowned night herons, great blue herons, great egrets, American white pelicans and eared grebes.

↑ **Many different types of warblers, such as magnolia warblers, visit Duck Mountain Provincial Park.**

↓ **Native to North America, the pileated woodpecker is a large woodpecker that is easily identified by its red crest and can be found in deciduous forests.**

## Duck Mountain Provincial Park

As the name suggests, Duck Mountain Provincial Park is home to a large number of waterfowl, including ducks. You'll find canvasbacks, mallards, ruddy ducks, northern pintails and more.

Besides water dwellers, the area in and around the park is the summer home for some of the most coveted songbirds that visit the boreal forest each year. This includes plenty of warblers, such as Blackburnian, magnolia and Nashville warblers. Other notable visitors include the great-crested flycatcher, veery, rose-breasted grosbeak and yellow-bellied sapsucker. Year-round residents, such as pileated woodpeckers and ruffed grouse, can also be seen.

When visiting Duck Mountain, check out the 2-kilometre Woodland Trail, the advanced 4-kilometre Pelly Point Trail and the 1-kilometre barrier-free Boreal Forest Trail for the best birdwatching opportunities.

**Note:** Don't confuse this park with the identically named Duck Mountain Provincial Park across the border in Manitoba.

↑ **Birders can keep an eye out for yellow-headed blackbirds in the marshy areas of the Prairie to Pine Corridor.**

## Prairie to Pine Corridor

Farther north, locations along the Prairie to Pine Corridor of the Saskatchewan Birding Trail feature a variety of habitats, such as wetlands, forests, grasslands, parkland and hills. The birding trail is not a specific trail per se, but rather a network of nature hot spots that attract a good number of birds each year. This selection also features several key migration spots.

Find six walking tours, and look for over 250 species that frequent the pristine freshwater lake region of St. Walburg. Standouts to see include orange-crowned warblers, Forster's terns and endangered whooping cranes.

Nearby Paradise Hill lives up to the beauty its name suggests. Boreal forests, wetlands, aspen woodlands and meadows attract diverse bird species. Expect to see great blue herons, white pileated woodpeckers, thrushes, rails and raptors, such as eagles and hawks.

The Turtle Lake and Livelong area is a breeding location for 150 species, including 13 types of warblers. Mervin, Edan and Vawn are also bird-rich areas that attract a large variety of birds each year and should not be missed.

# Common and Unique Animal Species

↑ **Found in the mid-boreal upland, timber wolf packs can cover a range of over several hundred kilometres.**

Thanks to so many ecoregions within Saskatchewan, the province hosts a great diversity of species, with over 70 species of mammals alone. Mammals range from tiny to massive and likely to unexpected. Whether you're driving along a prairie road, hiking a backwoods trail, canoeing on a lake or simply strolling in the city, you'll be surprised by the amount of wildlife to see in the province.

In addition to the variety of mammals, many of which cross over several parts of the province, there are some pretty unique species of all animal classes found in Saskatchewan.

## North

The north is home to a number of residents, such as black bears, wolves, moose, muskrats, beavers and snowshoe hares, that are commonly spotted from the mid-boreal upland up to the Selwyn Lake upland, northwest of the Churchill River.

Over the five northern ecoregions, however, there are other less-common species, such as timber wolves, lynx, red-backed voles, martens, and woodland and barren-ground caribou.

Other neat species found in the north include wolverines, which travel between the boreal forest and alpine tundra, and arctic foxes, which can be found in the upper northwest area of the province.

## Central

From the mid-boreal lowland, south of the Canadian Shield

↑ **Lynx, found in central and northern Saskatchewan, have large feet covered by dense, coarse hair that helps them travel over snow.**

and down to the boreal transition zone, the central region possesses a similar list of species to the north, such as moose, black bears, beavers, lynx and otters. Unlike in the north, elk can be found in the mid-boreal.

Moving farther south into the boreal transition ecoregion, white-tailed deer, coyotes and cottontail rabbits begin to appear. Hiking popular trails in and around areas like Prince Albert National Park often provides the opportunity to see an abundance of wildlife.

Other interesting, though rather hard-to-spot, species in this area of the province include flying squirrels and fishers.

↑ Several species, such as burrowing owls, black-footed ferrets, rattlesnakes and even black widow spiders, use the deep burrows dug by black-tailed prairie dogs.

↓ Commonly spotted in the southern part of the province, the pronghorn antelope is the fastest land mammal in North America.

## South

The southern ecoregions, comprised of aspen parkland, moist and mixed grassland and cypress upland, contain many of the same mammals as the lower central region. White-tailed deer, coyotes, pronghorn antelopes, red foxes, badgers and a variety of squirrels can be spotted nearly everywhere in the south, including in protected parks, on open prairies and sometimes within urban centres.

Some rare species are concentrated in particular parts of the province, and Grasslands National Park is home to a few. The black-footed ferret is a species that was reintroduced to the park in 2009, and the park is the last spot in Canada that the adorable black-tailed prairie dog exists. Reptiles found in Grasslands include the endangered short-horned lizard and the prairie rattlesnake, the only venomous snake in the Prairies.

Speaking of snakes, Saskatchewan is home to nine species, including the hog-nosed snake, bull snake and smooth green snake. Other cool reptiles found in the south are the northern leopard frog, the western tiger salamander and the western painted turtle, to name a few.

Perhaps the most surprising southern resident is the northern or boreal scorpion. Found in the South Saskatchewan River Valley, it is the only type of scorpion found in Canada. Hunting at night, this scorpion uses a stinger with venom to paralyze its prey as well as defend itself, but it doesn't pose a threat to humans. Northern scorpions reach up to 5 centimetres long and have even evolved to survive winter by hibernating. Another surprising critter found in the south, within the Great Sandhills region, is the rare-to-spot (and nocturnal) Ord's kangaroo rat.

Plains bison can be viewed throughout the province but particularly in the following areas: Grasslands National Park, Prince Albert National Park, Buffalo Pound Provincial Park and the Old Man on His Back Prairie and Heritage Conservation Area, a 5,300-hectare parcel of grassland south of Swift Current.

↑ The prairie rattlesnake is one of nine snake species found in the province.

→ Northern scorpions have evolved to survive Canadian winters.

# Paddling

↑ **Fond du Lac River offers beautiful beaches, rapids, waterfalls and more.**

A little-known fact about Saskatchewan is that two-thirds of it is covered by forest and water. With over 100,000 lakes and 50 documented canoe routes, there's no shortage of waterways to explore. From streams and lakes to rapids and waterfalls, there are a wealth of options to choose from. The best online resource for route information is Canadian Canoe Routes (myccr.com).

Northern Saskatchewan is unquestionably a paddler's paradise, but the south of the province shouldn't be overlooked. Whether by kayak or canoe, spending time paddling major prairie rivers or remote northern waterways promises to be an adventure.

A few iconic portages have been highlighted in previous chapters. Find out about the trek to Grey Owl's Cabin in **Prince Albert National Park** on pages 164–5, and learn about the historic Methye Portage into **Clearwater River Provincial Park** on page 187. You can also find information on the **Churchill River** on page 184.

Here are a few other routes and locations in Saskatchewan where paddling is a popular pastime.

## Fond du Lac River

Consider a guided expedition to the remote Fond du Lac River, a waterway that flows northwest along Saskatchewan's Tazin Lake upland biome and features rapids, falls, beaches and more. If you're lucky, the northern lights may even make an appearance while you're in the area.

While paddling the river, be sure to visit Manitou Falls, where the river flows through a narrow limestone gorge — a definite highlight. For a fulfilling experience, camp between portages, spend time fishing the rich waters and keep your eyes open for wildlife along the river's edge.

## Kingsmere River

In Prince Albert National Park, just northwest of Waskesiu Lake, is the accessible Bagwa Canoe Route, which starts out from a launch on Kingsmere Lake. Paddlers can expect to

↑ Take in the beauty of the boreal forest when paddling along the Kingsmere River in Prince Albert National Park.

↑ **The South Saskatchewan River can be accessed from several boat launches within Saskatoon's city limits.**

spend approximately 7 to 10 hours on the water, though the trip can easily be stretched out overnight.

The route includes short portages as it loops through Bagwa, Lily and Clare lakes. Enjoy the peace of the quiet lakes, and watch for water birds, such as loons, red-necked grebes, great blue herons and blue-winged teals, along the Bagwa Channel, where yellow pond lilies bob above the water.

## North and South Saskatchewan Rivers

Both of the province's major prairie waterways, the North and South Saskatchewan rivers, present options for paddling. On a relaxed float across parkland and prairie regions, paddlers can follow routes that are rich in both Indigenous and fur trade history.

The South Saskatchewan River offers multiple access points, depending on how much time paddlers want to spend on the water. If you only have a few hours, try the 20-kilometre trek from the popular Fred Heal Canoe Launch to Saskatoon or the 25-kilometre journey to Saskatoon from Paradise Beach (access is found south of the city).

↑ **Along the Porcupine River, look for the Eye Cave, which can only be seen up close by water.**

Though often overlooked, the North Saskatchewan River is an ideal paddling destination. Just outside of Prince Albert, you can set out on an easy 60-kilometre route that ends at the Forks, the point where the North and South Saskatchewan rivers meet. The boat launch is found east of the Highway 2 bridge, on the south side of the North Saskatchewan River.

## Porcupine River

The experienced paddler will find a true challenge paddling the uber-remote Porcupine River, where portaging woodland trails is required. Great challenges reap great rewards: spectacular shorelines, Precambrian granite cliffs, caves (like the dramatic Eye Cave), waterfalls and rapids make this wilderness area a paddler's utopia.

The 190-kilometre journey starts at Selwyn Lake, bordering the Northwest Territories, and ends at Black Lake. Travelling southwest into the Fond du Lac River, paddlers will be met with stretches of challenging rapids interspersed with expanses of fast-moving currents. Anglers should pack their rods, as trophy fish can be caught in the rapids above the waterfalls.

# Sky Viewing

↑ **Seeing the northern lights in the province can be done most anywhere in Saskatchewan, though chances are higher the farther north you travel.**

→ **The northern lights are spectacular over La Ronge.**

Whether it's finding the darkest spot with the most stars, taking in a sunrise or sunset, or searching for the aurora borealis, Saskatchewan's wide-open plains offer sky-viewing opportunities that are hard to beat.

One thing that's true about Saskatchewan — the skies are pretty brilliant no matter where you are. Skies filled with stars and swirls of green can be seen province-wide — yes, even from within city limits. It's for these reasons the province is known as the "Land of Living Skies." However, a few places in particular stand out as prime sky-viewing and stargazing areas.

## North

Though you can see the aurora borealis in the south and central parts of the province, heading north will further increase your odds of catching a spectacular multicoloured light show.

With 11 provincial parks north of Saskatoon, there are many spots where you can keep your eyes directed to the sky while on vacation. The best months for aurora viewing are October to March. Try a visit to Melfort in the province's northeast. It was once nicknamed the "City of Northern Lights" thanks to how frequently they appear.

Farther north, Amisk Lake near Flin Flon, La Ronge, Missinipe and Stanley Mission are all great options. If you're lucky, you'll see the swirling green and purple hues dance on the water, as well.

## Central

Within the city limits of Saskatoon, there are a few optimal spots for night-sky and aurora viewing.

The Meewasin Valley Trail boasts 80 kilometres of trails that stretch through green spaces and offer several great areas to stop and stargaze. Suggested spots include most anywhere along the riverbank trails, the Peggy McKercher Conservation Area and the Beaver Creek Conservation Area, which sits south of the city and hosts stargazing events.

Light pollution decreases the farther you get from city limits, so heading north of Saskatoon to Wanuskewin Heritage Park, Cathedral Bluffs or near the Clarkboro Ferry offers alternative spots for marvelling at the night sky.

↑ **Grasslands National Park offers unobstructed views of the sky, making sunsets spectacular.**

## South

A vast expanse of land covering 527 square kilometres, Grasslands National Park Dark-Sky Preserve is an ideal spot to be surrounded by the prairie skies. Whether it is morning or night, sunrise or sunset, the opportunity to feel completely surrounded by a 360-degree panorama makes sky viewing in the park amazing.

The area is perfect for stargazing because there is no light pollution in the area. As one of two Dark-Sky Preserves in the province and one of the darkest preserves in Canada, the park's skies actually shine brightest at night.

Unsurprisingly, it's a favourite spot for astronomers to gather — as is the province's other Dark-Sky Preserve, in Cypress Hills Interprovincial Park, about 120 kilometres northwest.

Cypress Hills, which stretches across the provincial border into Alberta, is one of

↑ Consider taking part in the annual Saskatchewan Summer Star Party at Cypress Hills Interprovincial Park.

Canada's most accessible Dark-Sky Preserves. Head for the observatory when visiting. Created in 2011, it includes a dome observatory with seating and telescope platforms. It's open from May long weekend to Labour Day.

Stargazing is serious business in the park (there's even a Dark-Sky Campground), and programming includes astronomy education and an Astronomer-in-Residence program. Additionally, every year in August the Saskatoon and Regina centres of the Royal Astronomical Society of Canada hold the Saskatchewan Summer Star Party, where all-night observing sessions are enjoyed.

Other spots in the southwest for prime sky viewing include the Avonlea Badlands (where Milky Way and Moonlight tours run during the summer months) and Castle Butte, both of which provide incredible foregrounds for the night sky.

# Waterfalls

↑ **At 15-metres tall, Hunt Falls is considered Saskatchewan's most impressive falls.**

One thing that astonishes many visitors to Saskatchewan is the diversity of its topography. From sand dunes and grasslands to boreal forests and Canadian Shield backdrops, the province offers a wide range of landscapes and natural geological features. That being said, there's another surprising natural attraction to add to the list: waterfalls.

With over 100,000 lakes and rivers, it shouldn't come as a shock that the province is home to its share of waterfalls, both large and small. But then again, it may be surprising since many people associate the province with golden fields rather than beautiful waterways. Most of the falls can be found in the remote northern parts of the province, deep within the Canadian Shield.

Note that extra caution should be taken when hiking near waterfalls, especially if the area is rocky or looks slippery. Ice formations at waterfalls and near water, while photogenic, can be dangerous.

## Hunt Falls

Considered Saskatchewan's most beautiful falls by many, Hunt Falls, found in the northwest, is also the highest in the province. Standing 15 metres high and 60 metres wide, the falls are a part of a dramatic section of the mighty Grease River that drops 35 metres in 3 kilometres.

Grease River flows from close to the border with the Northwest Territories southwards into Lake Athabasca. Though remote, you can access the area via float plane from Stony Rapids.

## Nistowiak Falls

The Cree word *nistowiak*, meaning "meeting of the waters," suits these falls perfectly. Find the Nistowiak Falls in Lac La Ronge Provincial Park, where Lac La Ronge meets (or rather drains into) the Churchill River by flowing from the higher-level Iskwatikan Lake into Nistowiak Lake.

Noted as one of the highest falls in Saskatchewan, these impressive 10-metre falls are accessible by boat or

float plane. Boat tours can be arranged in Stanley Mission, or visitors can access the falls by canoe from Stanley Mission by paddling 20 kilometres east on the Churchill River.

In addition to Nistowiak Falls, the Churchill River is home to several other waterfalls, including Twin Falls, Robertson Falls and Kettle Falls. Kettle Falls, found tucked into the wilderness of the Canadian Shield, has a total drop of 5 metres and a width of 134 metres.

## Manitou Falls

A favourite among paddlers, Manitou Falls is the prominent feature of the Fond du Lac River and can be accessed via canoe. Other rapids and falls are found along the Fond du Lac River, which flows between Wollaston Lake and Stony Rapids, including Thompson Rapids and Burr Falls. The area is only accessible by a guided paddling trip or float plane.

↑ **Manitou Falls is the crown jewel of the Fond du Lac River.**

# Acknowledgements

We would like to respectfully acknowledge that many of the incredible nature hot spots mentioned in this book sit in the traditional territories of the First Peoples of Canada, who were truly the original stewards of this land's natural treasures.

We would like to extend special thanks to Tourism Saskatchewan, Saskatchewan Parks, the Royal Saskatchewan Museum, Nature Saskatchewan, Chaplin Nature Centre, Tourism Manitoba, Manitoba Parks, Watchable Wildlife Manitoba, Manitoba Conservation, Parks and Protected Spaces Branch of Manitoba, Nature Manitoba, Trails Manitoba, Churchill North, Churchill Northern Studies Centre, Churchill Wild Parks, Ontario Parks, Destination Ontario, Parks Canada, the Trans-Canada Trail Foundation (The Great Trail), Destination Canada (formerly the Canadian Tourism Commission), the Indigenous Tourism Association of Canada, the Canadian Wildlife Federation and Bird Canada.

Also a big shout out to the many talented and passionate outfitters, regional tourism boards, nature enthusiasts and Saskatchewan- and Manitoba-based photographers for their photo contributions.

# Photo Credits

Aaron Spence: 127 (top)
Alamy
    Alan Dyer/Stocktrek Images: 71;
    Alan Dyer/VW Pics: 211;
    blickwinkel/Teigler: 154;
    Dennis Fast/VW Pics: 65 (top), 72;
    Don Johnston_MA: 2–3, 67;
    Historic Collection: 92;
    Igor Smoljan: 50;
    Jason Doucette: 129, 157 (top);
    Jill Cooper: 210;
    Jordana Meilleur: 45 (top);
    Ken Gillespie/Design Pics Inc: 81;
    Ken Gillespie Photography: 49 (bottom), 155 (top)
    Mauro Toccaceli: 49 (top), 84;
    Mcmaster Studio: 89;
    Mike Grandmaison/Jaynes Gallery/
        DanitaDelimont.com: 52–53 (top), 59
        (top);
    Rick and Nora Bowers: 125 (bottom);
    Skip Moody/Dembinsky Photo Associ-
        ates: 53 (bottom), 58;
    Thomas Fricke/First Light: 19 (top)
Andrew Hiltz: 180, 181 (top)
Andy Goodson: 146–47, 148, 149 (top), 149 (bot-
    tom), 155 (top)
Angel Laliberte: 176–77 (top), 183 (top), 183
    (bottom)
Ashlyn George: 101 (top), 191 (bottom)
Bryan Mierau: 133
City of Yorkton: 139 (top), 139 (bottom)
Corey Hardcastle Photography: 194–95, 209
Destination Canada: 11, 29 (top), 29 (bottom), 37
    (top), 41, 68, 69, 70 (top), 70 (middle)
Destination Ontario: 12–13, 20, 21 (top), 32,
    33, 88
dsTroyer.ca/David S. Troyer (Courtesy of
    Tourism Moose Jaw): 135 (top)
Gary Bergen (Courtesy of Watrous Manitou
    Marketing Group): 132
Hap Wilson: 66, 91
Hilda Maier: 113
iStock
    Dougall_Photography: 168;
    IanChrisGraham: 25 (top), 94, 95, 103 (top);
    Mark_Norman: 203 (bottom);
    mysticenergy: 62, 63 (top), 63 (bottom);
    pac9012: 203 (top);
    sprokop: 172;
    vovamir: 85
Jeanine Holowatuik: 175 (bottom)
Jenn Smith Nelson: 102, 103 (bottom), 108, 109
    (top), 110, 111 (top), 111 (bottom), 115 (top),
    115 (bottom), 120, 122 (top), 123 (top), 123
    (bottom), 124, 142 (bottom), 143 (top), 165
    (top), 202 (top)
Jim Baird: 207
John Kindrachuk: 167 (top)

John Stead: 137 (bottom), 167 (bottom), 198
    (top), 199
Lawrence Donley: 60
Martin Kehoe: 61 (top)
Maxine Earl: 196, 197
Michael Murchison: 5, 97, 100, 101 (bottom), 105
    (top), 105 (bottom), 112, 116, 125
Natascha Thoennes: 188, 189 (top), 189 (bottom)
Nick Saunders: 182, 198 (bottom), 200, 202
    (bottom)
Oak Hammock Marsh Interpretive Centre: 26,
    27 (top), 27 (bottom)
Ontario Parks: 30, 31 (top), 43 (top),
Parks Canada: 36, 39, 77 (top);
    Glen and Rebecca Grambo: 163 (bottom);
    Greg Huszar: 164 (bottom), 205;
    Karyne Jolicoeur: 77 (bottom);
    Kevin Hogarth Photography: 163 (top),
        164 (top)
    L. Owen Knox: 121 (bottom)
Robin and Arlene Karpan: 56, 57 (bottom), 186,
    187, 204, 214–15
Rob Wright (Courtesy of the Ministry of Parks,
    Culture and Sport): 179 (bottom)
Ruth Hovdebo: 192, 193
Ryan Wunsch: 117 (bottom)
Shutterstock
    Alexander Kolikov: 128 (top);
    AndreAnita: 76;
    Beth Swanson: 107 (bottom);
    BGphotoaesthetics: 31 (bottom);
    BGSmith: 109 (bottom), 122 (bottom), 128
        (bottom left);
    Bob Bors: 151;
    Brian Lasenby: 31 (middle);
    Carmen Rieb: 24;
    Cindy Creighton: 38, 83 (top), 83 (bottom);
    Collins93: 25 (bottom), 111 (middle);
    Daniel Hussey: 16, 17 (bottom);
    David Unger: 181 (bottom);
    Delmas Lehman: 51 (top);
    Double Brow Imagery: 35 (bottom);
    Elena Elisseeva: 44;
    FotoRequest: 43 (bottom);
    Frenchwildlifephotograher: 61 (bottom);
    George Stone: 98–99, 121 (top);
    Hare Island Photography: 21 (bottom);
    Hayley Crews: 40;
    Hihatimages: 170;
    islavicek: 15 (bottom);
    Jacob Boomsma: 15 (top);
    Jeffrey Wiles: 19 (bottom);
    Jen Eden: 147 (top), 161 (bottom);
    Jim Cumming: 73;
    John Krampl: 46;
    Josef Pittner: 155 (bottom);
    Jpiks: 153 (top);
    Jukka Palm: 22;

Karel Bock: 141 (bottom);
kavram: 78–79, 87, 90;
Keith Levit: 37 (bottom);
Kerry Hargrove: 166;
Lorraine Swanson: 14;
Lost Mountain Studio: 131 (top);
M. Leonard Photography: 175 (top);
Matt Jeppson: 18, 45 (bottom);
Michelle Lalancette: 35 (top);
mmcool: 117 (top);
Nancy Bauer: 131 (bottom), 174;
Paul Reeves Photography: 34, 152;
Pictureguy: 130, 135 (bottom), 145 (middle),
    145 (bottom), 165 (bottom);
RAphoto77: 169;
RobHamm: 51 (bottom);
RRichard29: 80;
Sergey Uryadnikov: 59 (bottom);
Steve Cordory: 147 (middle), 157 (middle);
Steve Jamsa: 138;
Sylvie Bouchard: 47 (bottom);
vagabond54: 82;
Warren Metcalf: 201;
Wildnerdpix: 42;
wlkellar: 65 (bottom), 70 (bottom), 74
Tourism Estevan: 106
Tourism Regina: 141 (top), 142 (top), 143 (bottom)
Tourism Saskatchewan:
    Chris Hendrickson Photography: 184, 185
        (top), 185 (bottom);
    Davin Andrie: 212;
    Greg Huszar Photography: 119, 159
        (bottom), 160, 161 (top), 213;
    Kevin Hogarth Photography: 128 (right),
        137 (top);
    Larry Goodfellow: 208;
    Paul Austring: 119 (top), 127 (bottom), 144,
        145 (top), 153 (bottom), 159 (top), 190,
        191 (top);
    Saskatchewanderer: 150, 176–77 (bottom),
        178, 179 (top)
Tourism Saskatoon: 171, 173, 206
Travel Manitoba: 6–7, 17 (top), 23, 47 (top), 54, 55,
    57 (top), 75
Wikimedia Commons
    Danneufeldphoto [CC BY-SA 4.0 (https://
        creativecommons.org/licenses/by-
        sa/4.0)];
    Robert Linsdell from St. Andrews, Can-
        ada [CC BY 2.0 (https://creativecom-
        mons.org/licenses/by/2.0)]
Woodlawn Regional Park: 107 (top)

Front cover: Pictureguy/Shutterstock

Back cover (top to bottom): mysticenergy/
    iStock, AndreAnita/Shutterstock, IanChris-
    Graham/iStock

# Index for Manitoba

Note: Page numbers in **bold** refer to photographs.

# Index for Saskatchewan

Note: Page numbers in **bold** refer to
    photographs.

# Explore Canada's Nature Hot Spots with These Titles

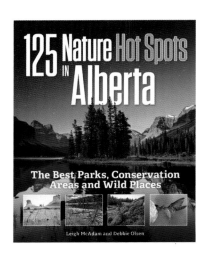

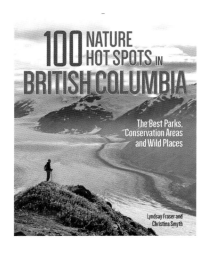

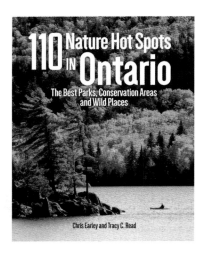

125 Nature Hot Spots in Alberta
ISBN: 978-0228100164

100 Nature Hot Spots in British Columbia
ISBN: ISBN: 978-0228100171

110 Nature Hot Spots in Ontario
ISBN: 978-0228100157

FIREFLY BOOKS